Hodder Gibson

D0434635

Scottish Examination Materials

HIGHER

FRENCH

Practice Papers

Reading and Directed Writing

Calum E. Ure, M.A. Hons

Hodder Gibson

2A Christie Street, Paisley, PA1 1NB

INTRODUCTION

This book is intended to help candidates prepare for the 80 hour unit of the Higher French examination. The material presented in this book gives candidates much needed practice in some of the tasks set at Higher level. I hope too that teachers and college lecturers will find this book a good source of relevant, topical and interesting materials to complement the Higher course.

Several of the Reading Tests in this book appeared in the first edition of *Practice Papers for Revised Higher French*. The passages, however, have since been shortened, modified and simplified to be an accurate reflection of what candidates can expect in the new Higher examination. The questions have been completely revised in keeping with the style of the new exam.

The book is divided into six parts: Reading Tests for preparation for the final exam, Answer Schemes, Directed Writing tasks, Phrases to help candidates prepare for Directed Writing, Reading Tests to prepare for the end of unit tests and Answer Schemes.

Acknowledgements

My grateful thanks to Isabelle Zaragoza for reading all the manuscript
and to the pupils of St. Columba's School, Kilmacolm, for trying out all the material.

Orders: please contact Bookpoint Ltd, 130 Milton Park, Abingdon, Oxon OX14 4SB. Telephone: (44) 01235 827720, Fax: (44) 01235 400454. Lines are open from 9.00 – 6.00, Monday to Saturday, with a 24 hour message answering service. You can also order through our website: www.hoddereducation.co.uk

British Library Cataloguing in Publication Data
A catalogue record for this title is available from The British Library

ISBN-10: 0-716-98016-9
ISBN-13: 978-0-716-98016-2

Published by Hodder Gibson, 2a Christie Street, Paisley PA1 1NB.
Tel: 0141 848 1609; Fax 0141 889 6315; email: hoddergibson@hodder.co.uk
First Published 2001
Impression number   10 9 8 7 6 5 4 3 2
Year   2009 2008 2007 2006 2005

Copyright ©2001 Calum E. Ure

Papers used in this book are natural, renewable and recyclable products. They are made from wood grown in sustainable forests. The logging and manufacturing processes conform to the environmental regulations of the country of origin.

Printed in Great Britain for Hodder Gibson, 2a Christie Street, Paisley, PA1 1NB, Scotland, UK by Martins of Berwick.

CONTENTS

READING

Advice to Teachers 4

Advice to Candidates 6

Reading — Lifestyles 8

Reading — Education and Work 23

Reading — The Wider World 41

Reading — Answer Schemes 53

DIRECTED WRITING

Advice to Candidates 83

Directed Writing 85

Directed Writing Phrases 95

END OF UNIT READING TESTS

Lifestyles 102

Education and Work 109

The Wider World 114

Answer Schemes 116

RECORDS OF ACHIEVEMENT 128

ADVICE TO TEACHERS

READING

The texts in this book are all taken from authentic French material. They are presented under three themes: Lifestyles, Education and Work and The Wider World. The texts are set alphabetically, not in order of difficulty. Each text has a section underlined for translation. I have provided a glossary after each text in which I have tried to include any words which may cause candidates difficulty or which do not appear in either the *Collins Pocket French*, the *Harrap French School* or the *Oxford Colour French* dictionaries.

As each of the texts relates directly to one of the themes, I suggest that candidates work through each section as they are studying that appropriate theme in class. In this way, the students are familiar with much of the vocabulary, and the text will help consolidate what the candidates already know as well as broaden their knowledge on that subject. Clearly, for candidates with less ability, a text directly related to the topic they are currently studying is more readily accessible to them.

At the start of the academic year when students are faced with longer pieces of prose for the first time, you may choose to work through a relevant text with the candidates. As the year goes on and candidates become more confident, you may decide that they can work on the texts independently and correct their own work. Certainly towards the end of the academic year, candidates should be able to tackle any of the texts on their own and feel a sense of achievement in their own accomplishment.

At stages during the year you may decide to set a text under exam conditions to see how well the candidates perform in the time given.

SPEAKING

Each of the texts can be exploited for speaking practice as they all relate to the Higher course themes and each one can be used as a stimulus for either group or class discussion. More able candidates can be asked to read a certain passage and can then be asked questions in French on the text to check their comprehension and initiate discussion.

DIRECTED WRITING AND DIRECTED WRITING PHRASES

All the Directed Writing topics require candidates to write using past tenses and often future or conditional tenses too. In the Directed Writing Phrases section, the phrases I have included are intended for candidates who are working without the constant help of a classroom teacher or lecturer. The phrases are divided up under headings and relate to a certain bullet point in one of the Directed Writing topics. Of course, candidates should be encouraged to use their own language, but if they do refer to the Directed Writing Phrases section, they should be encouraged to learn each new phrase so that it becomes part of their own language and can be successfully incorporated into another Directed Writing task at a later date.

As with the Reading texts, at appropriate stages during the year you may decide to set one of the Directed Writing topics as a forty minute test and impose exam conditions on the candidates.

END OF UNIT READING TESTS

I have included six Reading tests relating to the three themes of Lifestyles, Education and Work and The Wider World. These passages are shorter than the others, include more questions and do not contain a translation section. To pass, candidates have to achieve 60% of the total marks. You may wish to set candidates one of these prior to the end of unit test for extra practice. (As these Practice Papers are widely available, these tests will not be accepted as evidence that candidates have gained the unit award.)

ANSWER SCHEMES

Provided are answers to all of the questions and suggested translations. So that candidates do not feel disadvantaged, I have referred to the *Collins Pocket French*, the *Harrap French School* and the *Oxford Colour French* dictionaries and where appropriate I have used their suggested translations. After each End of Unit Reading Test I have indicated the unit award mark so that candidates can assess their own level of attainment.

Calum Ure

READING

ADVICE TO CANDIDATES

- Read the title and the English introduction.

- Read the text thoroughly before you begin, referring to the glossary.

- Read through all the questions as they reveal much about the text.

- Read the text a second time before starting the questions, looking up any words in the dictionary which impede your comprehension.

- Remember that the questions come in order. The answer to question 1 will be at the start of the text, the next answer will come after that, etc.

- A question worth 2 points requires two separate pieces of information, a question worth 3 points requires three separate pieces of information, etc. However, bear in mind that 1 point may be awarded for understanding one word, e.g., *vers dix heures* (<u>about</u> ten o' clock).

- Read through all the questions in one group before starting to write your answers, e.g., 2 *(a)*, *(b)* and *(c)*. As the answers will all be in one section of the text, make sure you give the answers which correspond to the correct questions.

- Include as much information as possible in the time given but express yourself clearly.

- Read through your answer before moving on to the next question. Does it make perfect sense in English? Have you included enough information for the number of points?

- Although it may take you longer at the start of the Higher year, practise answering all the questions (and translation section) in one hour.

- Take a note of any new words or phrases which appeal to you and learn them. The wider your vocabulary, the better you will perform in the Reading (and the other papers in the Higher examination).

- If you are having difficulty with one question, move on to the next and come back to it at the end.

TRANSLATION

ADVICE TO CANDIDATES

- Read the underlined section carefully and try to make sense of it before starting to write.

- Read what comes before and after the translation section so that you can put the section into context.

- In translating each word literally it may not sound English. The difficulty is always in remaining faithful to the sense of the French and in conveying this naturally in English. Watch out for the use of '*on*', e.g., *On va à la mer*. '<u>One</u> goes to the seaside' sounds stilted. A more natural translation would be '<u>We</u> go to the seaside'. Once you understand the phrase and it makes perfect sense in English, write it down. Read it again. If it sounds stilted or unnatural, you will have to alter it in some way.

- Identify all the verbs and recognise the correct tense.

THE MARKING OF THE READING AND TRANSLATION

The comprehension questions are worth 20 marks and the translation is worth 10 marks.

In your answers in the Reading it is important that you show your comprehension of the text, and that you can convey this factual information with as much detail and accuracy as possible. The number of points for each question corresponds to the number of points you have to write down from the text. On occasion, certain questions may be worth less than the number of points you can take from the text, e.g., a question may be worth 3 points but there may be 5 separate pieces of information in the text. You only have to write down 3 correct points. If you are in doubt about any of the points you are making in your answer, play safe and include at least one of the other points to be sure of getting 3 points.

Each of the translation sections is divided into 5 'sense units'. Two possible marks are awarded to each unit. If your translation of a unit is 'good', you will be awarded 2 marks. If your translation is satisfactory, you will given 1 mark. No marks are awarded for an 'unsatisfactory' translation. In simple terms, if you fail to demonstrate sufficient understanding or mistranslate, you gain no marks. If your translation conveys your comprehension but is imprecise, you will be awarded 1 mark. If your translation is precise and is conveyed clearly, you will receive 2 marks for that 'sense unit'.

READING

LIFESTYLES

Passage 1

Read the article carefully, then answer **in English** the questions which follow it.
You may use a French dictionary.

This article is about a young man's addiction to drugs and how he finally overcame his dependency.

J'ai plongé à 17 ans

Je suis né dans une famille sans problèmes financiers. Nous habitions un beau quartier de Paris. Mon père était très autoritaire. Je n'avais le droit de rien faire. Je ne pouvais pas aller jouer au foot avec mes copains, ni les amener à la maison. Ça, c'était interdit. Le pire, c'est que mon père ne justifiait jamais ses décisions. «C'est comme ça», disait-il.
5 Je trouvais cela stupide, injuste, révoltant. J'ai fini par croire que j'étais différent des autres.

Une chose était insupportable: nous ne parlions jamais, ou alors nous parlions de choses insignifiantes; «Tu as rangé ta chambre?», «Quelles notes as-tu eues à l'école aujourd'hui?» On ne parlait jamais de sujets graves. Je souffrais beaucoup de devoir
10 tout garder pour moi. A 9 ans, mon meilleur ami a déménagé. Ça a été un drame pour moi. Je n'ai pu en parler à personne.

Si je suis tombé dans la drogue, je pense, c'est pour me créer une nouvelle famille. J'avais besoin de gens avec qui je pourrais parler. C'était l'époque des hippies (la fin des années 60). Leur mode de vie m'attirait. Un copain m'avait dit qu'il pouvait se procurer du hasch.
15 J'ai eu envie d'essayer. En fait, ça m'a rendu complètement malade: j'ai eu très mal à la tête, j'ai vomi horriblement . . .

A 17 ans, j'ai eu une grosse déception amoureuse. Mon père a eu cette repartie très originale: «Une de perdue, dix de retrouvées[1] . . . » Et notre conversation s'est arrêtée là. Je me sentais très seul.

20 Après le bac, j'ai commencé à étudier la comptabilité mais je n'allais pas régulièrement au cours. La seule recherche qui m'intéressait, c'était moi. Puis tout est allé très vite. Un soir de Noël, un copain m'a proposé un acide, du LSD. J'ai essayé. J'avais tellement envie de tout oublier . . . C'était juste ce qu'il me fallait pour m'oublier. J'en prenais avec les copains, ou seul à la maison. Mes parents ont mis trois ans à s'en rendre compte.

25 C'est alors que j'ai rencontré une fille qui prenait de l'héroïne. On est sortis ensemble, et je suis devenu héroïnomane. Nora est tombée enceinte[2], elle continuait à se shooter. J'étais

fou de joie d'avoir un enfant. Je travaillais dans la journée, je dealais un peu pour payer la dope. Je pensais vraiment qu'on pouvait être toxicomane[3] et élever un enfant en même temps. Nora n'était pas d'accord. On s'est séparés, et j'ai gardé l'enfant, Julien.

30   En 1984, à 26 ans, j'ai rencontré Patricia. Elle nous a hébergés, Julien et moi. Elle nous héberge encore aujourd'hui! C'est elle qui m'a sauvé. Elle a joué pour moi le rôle d'une infirmière, d'une thérapeute, d'une mère. Effectivement, ça a duré six ans. Peut-être n'avais-je pas vraiment envie de guérir[4]. Jusqu'à un soir de Noël où Julien n'avait rien à manger: tout l'argent était parti en dope. J'ai eu tellement honte, il fallait vraiment que
35   j'arrête.

J'avais touché le fond. J'ai décidé alors de vivre. J'ai rencontré un psychiatre et je n'ai jamais repiqué. Et je ne le ferai pas. La drogue n'a plus rien à m'apprendre. Et puis parce que j'ai un projet: reconstituer une famille, élever mon fils, regagner sa confiance. Je suis pour lui le pire et le meilleur exemple. Le pire pour être tombé aussi bas, et le meilleur
40   pour m'en être sorti.

[1]   une de perdue, dix de retrouvées: 'plenty more fish in the sea'
[2]   enceinte: pregnant
[3]   un / une toxicomane: a drug addict
[4]   guérir: to get better, to be cured

QUESTIONS

1. We are we told about the author's family background.

    (a) Mention two things.   **2 points**

    (b) What two specific restrictions did his father impose on him as a child?   **2 points**

2. A major event happened in the author's life when he was 9.

    (a) What was it?   **1 point**

    (b) Why was this particularly traumatic for him?   **1 point**

3. The author started taking drugs (lines 12–16).

    (a) What reasons for this does he give?   **2 points**

    (b) Why was his first experience not a happy one?   **2 points**

4. He went to university.
    What evidence is there that he was not interested in his studies?   **1 point**

5. He started going out with Nora (lines 25–29).
    After the birth of his child, why did he and Nora split up?   **3 points**

6. The author met Patricia (lines 30–35).
    What happened one Christmas which finally prompted him to give up drugs for
    good?   **2 points**

7. The author has learned a lot from his experiences (lines 36–40).

    (a) What is his plan for the future?   **2 points**

    (b) Why does he consider himself the best and worst role model for his son?   **2 points**

                                                                                        (20 points)

                                                                                        = 20 marks

8. Translate into English:

    "Une chose était . . . garder pour moi."   (lines 7–10)   **10**

                                                                                        (30)

Passage 2

Read the article carefully, then answer **in English** the questions which follow it.
You may use a French dictionary.

This article is about Florence's changing relationship with her mother.

Je ne supporte plus ma mère

Depuis que je suis rentrée de vacances, je ne supporte plus ma mère, ni sa présence, ni le
son de sa voix, ni même ce qu'elle a à dire. C'est d'autant plus[1] étonnant que jusqu'à
présent, ma mère était tout pour moi. Quand elle parlait, je buvais ses paroles. Pour moi,
elle avait toujours raison et elle savait tout. Si elle avait le moindre[2] conflit avec mon père,
5 ou dans son travail, je pensais que c'était elle qui avait raison, toujours, toujours. Moi-
même je lui demandais conseil pour tout. Et je l'écoutais. D'ailleurs, j'avais une véritable
adoration pour elle. Et puis maintenant, crac! Elle m'énerve.

Tenez l'autre jour, elle m'appelle du bas de l'escalier: «Florence, descends, j'ai à te parler.
Ton frère a écrit, viens voir. Je vais te lire la lettre.» . . . Je ne sais pas ce qui m'a pris, je me
10 suis mise à hurler en me bouchant les oreilles. <u>Je suis descendue et je suis sortie en courant
de la maison. J'ai même couru dans la rue, comme si je me sauvais d'elle . . . Mais bien sûr
elle ne me courait pas après . . .</u> Puis j'ai marché jusqu'au bord du lac. Et, arrivée là, je me
suis mise à pleurer. Je me suis même dit que je ne devais pas avoir de telles réactions envers
ma mère. Après tout, qu'est-ce qu'elle m'a fait? Mais quand je suis rentrée, elle
15 m'a demandé, «Alors, tu t'es calmée?»

Quand je pense que l'année dernière seulement, j'étais encore si fière d'elle . . . Les fois où,
par exemple, elle venait me chercher à la sortie du collège! Mes copines me disaient: «Elle
est belle, ta mère, et jeune. Et puis qu'est-ce qu'elle s'habille bien!»

Il faut vous dire qu'à la maison, ça a toujours été comme ça: ma mère règne sur tout et sur
20 tout le monde. Elle est dynamique. Elle tranche, elle parle beaucoup, elle rit . . . et les gens
sont autour d'elle comme des mouches autour d'un pot de miel. Elle a des opinions sur
tout: l'éducation des enfants, les méthodes pédagogiques, la médecine. Jusqu'à présent, je
l'ai toujours écoutée bouche bée[3]. Mais maintenant je ne peux plus. Je ne sais pas ce qui
m'arrive.

25 C'est peut-être parce que j'ai passé quinze jours en vacances chez ma tante, la sœur de mon
père, qui est tellement différente de ma mère. Elle, elle parle très peu, mais elle est attentive
à tous ses enfants, à son mari et elle l'a été avec moi aussi pendant mon séjour chez eux.

J'aime beaucoup ma tante Madeleine. Quand on a besoin d'elle, elle est là comme par enchantement[4].

30 Au début, j'avais l'impression de vivre dans une planète inconnue. A table, tous les enfants parlent tous à la fois. Mais jamais ma tante ou mon oncle ne les interrompent, même quand ils disent des bêtises ou qu'ils ont des avis tout à fait différents de leurs parents. C'est chez eux que j'ai compris que toutes mes idées, toutes mes pensées, étaient celles de ma mère, et que je les exprimais avec autant d'assurance qu'elle. Un exemple: un jour ma tante
35 préparait une ratatouille[5].

«Tiens, lui dis-je, tu fais de la ratatouille avec de l'oignon?»

«Oui, pourquoi pas?»

«C'est de l'ail qu'il faut mettre.»

«C'est bon aussi avec de l'oignon.»

40 «Maman, elle met de l'ail.»

«Nous avons chacune nos méthodes. Tu me diras si ma ratatouille à l'oignon est bonne. D'accord? . . . »

Et elle était très bonne, sa ratatouille . . . à l'oignon!

Je ne sais pas pourquoi je vous raconte tout ça, mais il me semble qu'il y a un rapport avec
45 l'attitude que j'ai actuellement avec ma mère. L'autre jour, je me suis opposée à elle, plus pour le plaisir que par conviction. Elle disait:

«La photo "noir et blanc" ça, j'adore! La couleur, c'est vulgaire.»

«Moi, je préfère les photos en couleurs, ai-je dit, c'est cent fois plus beau, et plus vivant, et plus vrai. Une photo c'est un souvenir, pas nécessairement une œuvre d'art . . . »

50 Elle a été surprise de ma réaction.

«Qu'est-ce qui te prend[6]?»

«Il me prend, ai-je répondu, que je ne suis pas du tout de ton avis. C'est tout. Et que je le dis.»

[1] d'autant plus: all the more
[2] le moindre: the slightest
[3] bouche bée: flabbergasted
[4] comme par enchantement: as if by magic
[5] une ratatouille: a vegetable dish
[6] Qu'est-ce qui te prend?: What's up with you?

Questions

1. In the first paragraph Florence mentions the change in her relationship with her mother.

   (a) What is it about her mother she cannot stand? **2 points**

   (b) If her mother had an argument with Florence's father or at work, how did Florence react? **1 point**

2. Florence tells us about an incident she had with her mother recently (lines 8–15).

   (a) Why did her mother want her to come downstairs? **2 points**

   (b) How did Florence react upstairs to her mother's request? **2 points**

   (c) What did her mother ask her when she came back home? **1 point**

3. Florence used to be so proud of her mother.
   Why was this? **2 points**

4. In paragraph 4 Florence describes her mother's behaviour at home.

   (a) What is she like? **3 points**

   (b) Mention two things on which her mother has an opinion. **2 points**

5. Florence compares her mother to her Aunt Madeleine (lines 25–29).
   How do they differ? **2 points**

6. Florence mentions what it was like at first staying with her aunt (lines 30–34).
   What was the one thing Florence learned about herself? **2 points**

7. From your reading of the final paragraph, how would you sum up the change in Florence's behaviour? **1 point**

   (20 points)

   = 20 marks

8. Translate into English:

   "Je suis descendue et . . . courait pas après . . ."   (lines 10–12). **10**

   (30)

Passage 3

Read the article carefully, then answer **in English** the questions which follow it.
You may use a French dictionary.

This article is about young people from different social backgrounds and how they spend Sunday.

Le dimanche des enfants

Elodie vient d'avoir 15 ans. Il y a deux sortes de dimanches, dit Elodie: ceux qui sont «ennuyeux parce que la famille se repose», et ceux qui sont excitants parce qu'elle les consacre à sa passion: le théâtre. Depuis l'âge de 7 ans, Elodie joue dans une troupe amateur. Pour elle, le dimanche il y a des répétitions et au bout de quelques semaines des
5   représentations[1]. «C'est le seul jour de la semaine où tout le monde est disponible en même temps.»

Olivia, 11 ans raconte: «Les dimanches, c'est la forêt, c'est s'échapper de Nice.» Sa famille se partage une vieille et grande maison de village en montagne. «C'est comme des vacances. Les parents oublient d'être sur notre dos pour nous dire: "C'est l'heure, fais tes
10   devoirs, dépêche-toi." Au printemps il y a les longues parties de *Monopoly* avec papa et les châtaignes que l'on cherche sous les feuilles en automne.» Et aussi «les matins glacés d'hiver où l'on part les skis sur le dos. Et puis les rentrées tardives à la maison, et maman qui dit: "Nous sommes encore rentrés trop tard. Mangez vite, il est temps d'aller au lit."»

Élève de sixième à Vénissieux, Ludovic, 12 ans, tape dans le ballon devant son HLM[2].
15   «Le dimanche, on fait ce qu'on veut.» La journée est plus intéressante pourtant quand il y a assez de copains pour organiser un match de football. Le dimanche apporte même parfois un peu d'air frais, quand ses parents se rendent[3] dans un jardin ouvrier qu'ils louent. Ludovic les accompagne mais les regarde travailler plus qu'il ne les aide: «J'aime bien arroser, mais arracher les carottes, ça non!»

20   Et puis il y a les enfants qui s'ennuient parce que leurs parents travaillent, comme Obé, dont le papa est chauffeur de taxi. «Mes parents veulent dormir, et je n'ai pas le droit de faire du bruit ou d'inviter mes copains», regrette-t-il. Alors, tout compte fait, ces enfants-là préfèrent encore l'école au dimanche et attendent le lundi avec impatience. Comme Mathieu, 13 ans, au collège Joffre de Montpellier: «Un dimanche sur quatre, je passe
25   l'après-midi devant la télé. Pour tuer le temps, je zappe à la recherche d'un bon film. Sur le câble, il y a une chaîne qui s'appelle Ciné-Cinémas. C'est celle que je regarde le plus souvent, mais il faut que le film soit bon, c'est-à-dire que ce soit un film d'action, sinon, je regarde des cassettes: *Alien*, *Terminator*. Par contre, je n'aime pas Sylvester Stallone; je trouve que ce n'est pas un bon acteur. Je n'aime pas sa façon de parler et il se prend trop au
30   sérieux.»

* subjunctive

14

Pour les enfants du divorce, comme Marie, 13 ans, élève dans un collège dans le Rhône, l'année est rythmée par les dimanches avec papa, et ceux avec maman. «Maintenant, je fais deux fois plus de choses qu'avant. Le dimanche avec maman, on va au cinéma, et l'hiver, on fait du ski avec une association. Quand c'est le tour de papa, je l'accompagne à
35   son club d'aviation, ou alors on marche ensemble dans les Alpes.»

Et que pensent les parents des week-ends? «J'en ai marre des piscines bondées[4] ou du zoo où on connaît par cœur tous les animaux pour les avoir fréquentés depuis trois ans, un dimanche sur deux. *Euro Disney* devrait être gratuit pour les parents. Vous croyez que ça m'amuse, la queue devant les guichets ou la bousculade pour voir la grande parade? Après
40   tout, j'ai aussi le droit de m'amuser le dimanche.»

[1]   une représentation: a performance
[2]   un HLM: a council flat
[3]   se rendre: to go
[4]   bondé: crowded

Questions

1. Read the first paragraph. What two kinds of Sunday might Elodie have? Give
    details.   **2 points**

2. Olivia's weekends are different (lines 7–13).

    (a) Where does she go?   **2 points**

    (b) Why does it feel like going on holiday?   **1 point**

    (c) Mention 3 activities she does there at different times of the year.   **3 points**

3. Ludovic comes from Vénissieux, a deprived part of Lyon (lines 14–19).

    (a) How does he occupy himself on his own?   **1 point**

    (b) What does he do if enough of his friends are available?   **1 point**

    (c) What does he tell us about helping his parents on their allotment?   **3 points**

4. Mathieu spends a lot of time in front of the television (lines 23–30).
    What does he not like about Sylvester Stallone?   **2 points**

5. Read paragraph 5.

    (a) In what way has the divorce of Marie's parents had a positive effect on her
          Sundays?   **1 point**

    (b) What does she do with her father?   **2 points**

6. From the final paragraph, mention two things this particular parent does not enjoy
    at *Euro Disney*?   **2 points**

                                                                                     (20 points)

                                                                                     = 20 marks

7. Translate into English:

    "Et puis . . . inviter mes copains." (lines 20–22)   **10**

                                                                                     (30)

Passage 4

Read the article carefully, then answer **in English** the questions which follow it.
You may use a French dictionary.

This passage is about the relationship between a father and his daughter.

Mon père ne veut pas me laisser vivre ma vie

Le carnet de notes d'Olivia est très impressionnant: 18 sur 20 en maths, 15 sur 20 en physique, 17 sur 20 en histoire. Depuis la classe de sixième, son père exige qu'elle se maintienne[1] en tête de la classe. «Il veut absolument que je réussisse dans la vie, dit-elle. Lui, il rêve que je sois avocate ou docteur et moi, je veux faire du théâtre!»

5 Bernard Morel fait tout pour que sa fille unique soit la meilleure. Elle doit assister aux cours du soir et il insiste pour qu'elle fasse des devoirs pendant les vacances. Cette année, c'est le baccalauréat. Sans la pression permanente que lui impose son père, Olivia passerait l'épreuve sans problème.

«Il a tellement peur que je ne sois pas la meilleure de la classe qu'il me stresse dès que je
10 rentre du lycée. J'ai l'impression qu'il n'a plus confiance en moi. Pourtant, je suis assez grande pour faire mes devoirs toute seule . . . »

La tension s'est accentuée[2] le jour où, à 15 ans, Olivia a fait un stage de théâtre. Elle éprouve de la fascination pour la scène. «Pour moi, c'était une révélation. J'ai décidé que je voulais devenir actrice. Je n'ai pas osé dire tout de suite à mon père que je voulais en
15 faire mon métier. J'ai d'abord lutté pour qu'il accepte que je m'inscrive aux cours de théâtre du lycée. Au début, il ne m'a pas du tout prise au sérieux. Il a pensé que ça me passerait. Et comme ma passion n'a fait que s'accentuer, ça a commencé à l'inquiéter! Tous les mardis soirs, après le cours, il boude. C'est un vrai gamin! Je m'en fiche, jamais je n'abandonnerai mon idée de devenir actrice. Je ferai tout pour avoir le bac et lui faire
20 plaisir; comme j'ai été habituée à travailler, ce sera facile, mais je n'accepterai pas de m'inscrire en faculté de droit ou de médecine! Quelle horreur! Ça ne m'intéresse pas!»

Bernard Morel n'accepte pas non plus que sa fille sorte avec n'importe qui. «Je préviens[3] mes amis avant qu'ils viennent chez moi! dit Olivia. Mon père juge mes copains en cinq minutes, sans prendre le temps de les connaître. Ils doivent venir à la maison avec un jean
25 propre et une chemise repassée, dire "bonjour monsieur" et se présenter au téléphone!»

Sa mère l'a bien compris, d'ailleurs. C'est elle qui trouve les meilleurs alibis pour que sa fille puisse sortir s'amuser de temps en temps, sans créer de drame à son retour. «La semaine dernière, elle a raconté à mon père que j'étais en train de bosser mes maths avec une copine alors que j'étais allée voir une pièce de théâtre. On est toujours obligées de lui
30 mentir, et c'est regrettable! J'ai déjà essayé de lui parler, mais il ne m'écoute jamais!»

Mais lorsque, l'été dernier, son père décide de l'inscrire contre son gré pour un stage d'un mois en Angleterre, elle se rebelle. «J'avais prévu de passer les vacances chez l'oncle d'une copine dans le Midi. Quand il m'a annoncé que je devrais partir à Liverpool pour améliorer mon anglais, c'était la haine! Je suis partie en claquant la porte, chez ma copine.
35 Le lendemain, on a pris le train ensemble pour Marseille et on est restées toutes les vacances chez son oncle. C'était génial! Et je n'ai donné aucune nouvelle.»

Au retour des vacances, l'autorité paternelle ressurgit[4]. «J'ai appris à prendre les choses avec humour. Grâce à ma mère, je peux ruser[5] pour sortir. Le plus dur sera de lui faire accepter l'idée que je veux m'inscrire dans une école de théâtre et de lui dire que j'ai déjà
40 réussi le concours d'entrée. Pour moi, c'est plus important que le bac. Je suis vraiment prête à tout, même à travailler dans un fast-food après les cours pour financer mes études. Ce sera la vie d'artiste!»

[1] se maintenir: to remain
[2] s'accentuer: to increase
[3] prévenir: to warn
[4] resurgir: to reappear
[5] ruser: to use cunning

Questions

1. Olivia gets very good marks at school.

    (a) What is the one thing that Olivia's father has demanded
         of her since first year?   **1 point**

    (b) What would her father like her to become?   **2 points**

2. Bernard Morel wants his daughter to be the best.
    What two things does Olivia have to do to please her father?   **2 points**

3. The tension between Olivia and her father increases when she finds her true
    vocation (lines 12–21).

    (a) When she started doing drama at school, how did her father react?   **2 points**

    (b) How does he behave now after her drama class at school?   **1 point**

4. Bernard Morel is very particular about Olivia's friends.

    (a) In what way is Olivia critical of him in this respect.   **2 points**

    (b) How does he expect her friends to dress?   **2 points**

5. Read paragraph 7.

    (a) Why did Olivia rebel against her father last summer?   **2 points**

    (b) What were her own plans?   **2 points**

    (c) On holiday, in what way did she punish her father?   **1 point**

6. In the final paragraph Olivia reveals her plans for the future.

    (a) What is going to be the most difficult thing for her?   **2 points**

    (b) What is she prepared to do to finance her studies?   **1 point**

                                                                              (20 points)

                                                                              = 20 marks

7. Translate into English:

    "La semaine dernière . . . c'est regrettable!"   (lines 27–30)   **10**

                                                                              (30)

19

Passage 5

Read the article carefully, then answer **in English** the questions which follow it.
You may use a French dictionary.

This article from a teenage magazine is about drinking too much at parties and gives the reader advice on how to avoid this.

On boit trop dans les fêtes

Une fête sans alcool, a-t-on jamais vu ça? Les soirées-limonade sont des événements rares. Dans un récent sondage 42% d'entre vous déclaraient avoir consommé au moins une boisson alcoolisée au cours des sept derniers jours; et parmi ceux-là, l'énorme majorité avait bu au cours d'une fête. Par ailleurs, un jeune sur trois déclare avoir été ivre . . .

5 «Le lundi matin, je vois souvent des élèves qui ont la gueule de bois[1]. Ils arrivent en retard et oublient d'apporter leurs affaires de classe. Ensuite, ils quittent les cours car ils ont mal à la tête ou ont mal au cœur», raconte une infirmière scolaire.

Bien sûr, on ne va pas vous défendre de boire la moindre goutte[2] d'alcool alors qu'on en trouve jusque sur la table familiale. Simplement, il faut apprendre à boire avec modération.

10 C'est vrai qu'un verre peut aider certains à se mettre dans l'ambiance de la fête, à leur éviter de rester seuls dans leur coin. Mais si vous buvez très régulièrement, et à haute dose, il est urgent de vous interroger: que cherchez-vous au fond de votre verre? Le courage d'inviter les filles à danser? La force de vous mêler aux conversations des autres? Sans doute un petit peu de tout ça. On boit pour faire comme les copains. Le verre à la main est
15 un signe d'intégration au groupe.

«A l'âge de quinze ans, j'ai été invitée à une fête, raconte Cécile. Il y avait de l'alcool et tout le monde en buvait. Moi, je savais que je ne supportais pas l'alcool mais pour faire comme les autres, j'ai bu n'importe quoi . . . J'ai fumé aussi, alors que je déteste ça. J'ai commencé à raconter n'importe quoi. C'est comme ça que j'ai passé le reste de la soirée
20 allongée sur le balcon. J'avais seulement la permission de 1h du matin mais à 4h, j'étais toujours à la fête. <u>Mon père est venu me chercher dans un état incroyable! Le pire, c'est que je lui ai raconté tout ce que j'avais dit et fait. Le lendemain, j'osais à peine le regarder en face. J'avais un mal de tête infernal.</u> En tout cas, c'est fini, je ne bois plus. Le but, c'est d'être responsable de soi et de ses actes.»

25 L'alcool fait courir des risques! Comme Cécile, vous pouvez donner une lamentable image de vous. Vous pouvez également être victime d'un accident de la route. Là, ça peut être grave. Et ça arrive tous les jours.

Alors, pour vous éviter de finir vos soirées à l'hôpital, rappelez-vous ceci: l'alcool passe directement dans le sang[3] en une heure et la désintoxication est longue puisqu'il faut trois
30 heures pour éliminer 3 verres d'alcool dans le sang. Adoptez la stratégie de Géraldine: «Je ne bois qu'un seul verre d'alcool; le reste de la soirée, je bois de l'eau minérale gazeuse.»

Évitez aussi les mélanges alcool-jus de fruits au alcool-soda, qui se boivent si facilement qu'on oublie la présence de l'alcool. Dosez vous-même votre verre, ça évitera les mélanges 50-50 qui sont dangereux. Si c'est vous qui organisez la fête, inventez des
35 cocktails sans alcool. Avec un peu d'imagination, on obtient des cocktails de fruits excellents. Un autre conseil: apprenez à partir à temps d'une fête, quand les copains commencent à attaquer le bar de papa. C'est souvent à ce moment-là que les choses dégénèrent. Enfin, mettez-vous d'accord[4], avant, pour qu'un membre du groupe au moins reste sobre: lui pourra éviter les bêtises de fin de soirée.

40 Et puis, entre nous, être capable de boire un jus d'orange sans vodka, n'est-ce pas aussi faire preuve de force de caractère et de maturité?

[1] avoir la gueule de bois: to have a hangover
[2] une goutte: a drop
[3] le sang: blood
[4] se mettre d'accord: to come to an agreement

Questions

1. In the first paragraph we are given information about young people and alcohol.

    (a) What did 42% of adolescents reveal in a recent survey?   **3 points**

    (b) What are we told about one in three of those surveyed?   **1 point**

2. According to the school nurse, why do some pupils leave the class?   **2 points**

3. The author suggests why young people drink at parties (lines 10–15).

    (a) How can alcohol help certain individuals?   **2 points**

    (b) According to the author, why do some people drink lots on a regular basis? **3 points**

4. Cécile tells us about a bad experience she had at a party (lines 16–24).

    (a) Why did she drink alcohol?   **1 point**

    (b) What two other things did she do which she regrets?   **2 points**

    (c) Where did she spend the rest of the evening?   **2 points**

5. The author suggests you follow Géraldine's example.
    What does she do?   **2 points**

6. The author gives the reader advice (lines 32–39).

    (a) When should you leave a party?   **1 point**

    (b) What should you agree on with your friends prior to the party?   **1 point**

                                                                                      (20 points)

                                                                                      = 20 marks

7. Translate into English:

    "Mon père est venu . . . mal de tête infernal."   (lines 21–23)   **10**

                                                                                      (30)

EDUCATION AND WORK

Passage 6

Read the article carefully, then answer **in English** the questions which follow it.
You may use a French dictionary.

This article is about the problems teachers face in motivating pupils.

C'est la rentrée!

Un élève de six ans qui pleure ou se rebelle dix minutes avant de partir en classe, c'est un enfant que l'école rend malheureux. Il déteste l'école car elle le sépare de ses parents, il en a peur. C'est très désagréable pour les parents, mais généralement après quelques semaines, l'enfant commence à s'adapter à son nouvel environnement.

5 L'élève "démotivé", c'est différent. Ni cris, ni larmes[1]: l'école ne lui fait pas peur, simplement il y va par habitude, pour voir les copains, parce qu'il faut bien aller quelque part. Mais quant à travailler, y faire des efforts, ou même simplement y écouter le cours, c'est une autre affaire. D'ailleurs, s'il trouve mieux à faire il n'hésitera pas à sécher[2] quelques cours ou même quelques jours.

10 Cette seconde attitude est aujourd'hui la plus inquiétante car elle semble se développer rapidement. On vient en effet d'apprendre que l'absentéisme[3] occasionnel concerne un élève sur deux, et un sur dix de manière régulière.

«Les élèves qui ne sont pas motivés c'est mon pain quotidien», soupire Odile, prof de maths dans un collège de Seine-Saint-Denis, toujours "stressée" au moment de faire son
15 premier cours malgré ses 17 ans d'expérience. «Beaucoup ont leurs parents au chômage, ils entendent parler de bacheliers qui arrivent tout juste à trouver un emploi comme caissier au supermarché. Comment est-ce que je peux leur parler d'un avenir radieux?»

C'est un fait: l'argument de l'importance des études sur le marché de l'emploi, longtemps argument "ultime" des profs comme des parents («passe ton bac d'abord») est moins
20 légitime. Mais que dire aux adolescents? Quel but leur proposer? Le plaisir d'apprendre? «L'essentiel de mon discours de rentrée, confirme Odile, consiste à leur apprendre à se lever en silence quand j'entre en classe et à ne pas oublier leurs livres et leurs cahiers.»

Comment encourager les jeunes? Seule la prof de secrétariat, Anne, l'a compris. «Si vous avez un problème, n'hésitez jamais à me demander de vous aider: s'il faut réexpliquer trois
25 fois, on le fera.» Quand on échoue à un examen, elle a toujours l'air surpris: «Eh bien, que vous est-il arrivé?» Avec elle, les élèves ont l'impression de valoir mieux que leurs notes. Elle leur fait confiance. Voilà le maître-mot: confiance. Les élèves aiment être traités comme des adultes et pas comme des "gamins".

Carole, prof d'espagnol, insiste simplement: «Vous avez été bon ou mauvais l'année
30   dernière je m'en fiche. Cette année on commence autre chose. Travaillons!» Elle montre
aussi un certain détachement; «Je prends mon sujet au sérieux, mais je ne me fâche pas si
deux élèves rigolent bêtement pendant que je leur parle de l'amour dans le roman *Don
Quichotte*. Sinon, c'est intolérable: on commence à trouver les élèves décevants et on finit
par[4] les mépriser. Je me dis simplement qu'on ne peut pas attendre des adolescents qu'ils
35   se passionnent pour tout, tout le temps.»

Mais il y a des profs qui souffrent beaucoup aussi à cause de la démotivation de leurs
élèves. Lucile, 17 ans, lycéenne à Paris raconte: «L'an passé, on a tout de suite senti que la
prof d'histoire-géo devait friser[5] la dépression. Elle a commencé l'année en tremblant
devant nous. Elle l'a finie en tremblant. Pendant ses cours on a plus joué aux cartes que pris
40   des notes.»

[1]   une larme: a tear
[2]   sécher: to skip
[3]   l'absentéisme: absenteeism
[4]   finir par: to end up
[5]   friser: to be on the verge of

Questions

1. Read the first paragraph. Give two reasons why some 6 year old pupils are unhappy
    at school.   **2 points**

2. A pupil lacking motivation is different.
    Why does he go to school?   **3 points**

3. Truancy is on the increase.
    What statistics are we given in the third paragraph concerning occasional and
    frequent absenteeism?   **2 points**

4. Odile has difficulty motivating her pupils (lines 13–22).

    (a)   Why does she find it so hard?   **3 points**

    (b)   What is the most important thing Odile wants to teach her pupils at the start of
            the school year?   **2 points**

5. Read paragraph 6.

    (a)   What does Anne say to encourage her pupils?   **3 points**

    (b)   How do pupils like to be treated?   **1 point**

6. Carole appears quite realistic (lines 29–35).
    What does she tell herself about adolescents?   **2 points**

7. In the final paragraph we are given Lucile's impression of her teacher.

    (a)   Why did she think her teacher was on the verge of a breakdown last year?   **1 point**

    (b)   What evidence is there that the pupils did not learn much?   **1 point**

                                                                                   (20 points)

                                                                                   = 20 marks

8. Translate into English:

    "Travaillons! . . . le roman de *Don Quichotte*." (lines 30–33)   **10**

                                                                                   (30)

Passage 7

Read the article carefully, then answer **in English** the questions which follow it.
You may use a French dictionary.

This article is about a day in the life of a hotel manager.

Directrice d'hôtel

A sept heures Annie Zorelle arrive à son hôtel-restaurant, un deux étoiles dans une petite ville entre Lyon et Grenoble. Annie, 42 ans, va d'abord saluer les clients qui prennent leur petit déjeuner. Un petit mot à chacun pour vérifier que tout se passe bien. Pour être satisfaite, la clientèle doit se sentir l'objet de toutes les attentions. Les habitués[1] sont traités
5 avec un soin particulier: «On discute de leurs projets pour la journée.» Puis elle s'installe à la réception pour accueillir les clients qui veulent régler leur note.

Ensuite Annie rejoint les deux femmes de chambre chargées de l'entretien des quinze chambres. «Je vérifie les réservations, le nombre de chambres libres. Et on définit celles qu'il faut nettoyer en priorité.» Chaque chambre est inspectée avec minutie. Rien de pire
10 qu'une ampoule grillée, une fuite, une télé défaillante pour ternir l'image de l'hôtel!

A dix heures le cuisinier arrive. La directrice revient avec lui sur[2] le service de la veille. «On discute de la qualité des plats, mais aussi des commentaires des clients.» Puis tous deux s'intéressent au menu du jour et le cuisinier dresse une liste des denrées dont il a besoin. Une fois par semaine, Annie se lève à 4 heures du matin pour s'approvisionner au
15 marché *Gar*, à Lyon. Un moment privilégié pour rencontrer ses fournisseurs et ses confrères: «On parle de la saison touristique, on compare, on discute aussi de ce qui se passe ailleurs dans la région.»

Vers une heure dans le restaurant, une dizaine de tables sont occupées. L'endroit jouit d'une bonne réputation. A part le chef, un commis[3] et un plongeur s'affairent en cuisine,
20 tandis que trois personnes servent dans la salle à manger. Annie fait le tour des tables. Toujours ce fameux souci de la clientèle.

Trois heures plus tard dans son bureau, situé juste derrière la réception, Annie s'affaire sur les comptes de l'établissement et classe des documents. Le chiffre d'affaires atteint en moyenne 10 000F par jour mais peut grimper jusqu'à 40 000F ou 50 000F si Annie
25 organise un banquet. Pas question de se tromper dans les additions . . . D'ailleurs, elle attend la visite de son comptable.

Le comptable arrive et ensemble, ils trient les factures à régler: électricité, téléphone, fournisseurs . . . Qui payer vite et en priorité? Puis ils abordent la question du remboursement d'un prêt bancaire souscrit pour rénover l'hôtel il y a quelques années. Le
30 taux d'intérêt doit pouvoir être renégocié avec le banquier. Un établissement comme celui d'Annie doit en permanence investir pour améliorer ses prestations[4] (mobilier, air conditionné, téléphone . . .) et rester dans la norme des deux étoiles.

A six heures du soir des clients interrogent Annie sur les lieux intéressants à visiter. Annie connaît bien sa région: elle recommande la visite du manoir ou bien encore celle de
35 l'entreprise artisanale qui fabrique des alcools de poire . . . Les premiers clients du restaurant arrivent. Chaleureuse, Annie propose la carte et dispense ses conseils. «J'ai une passion pour le vin. J'aime bien recommander certaines cuvées et expliquer aux clients l'histoire et les qualités de chaque cru.»

Vers minuit Annie termine ses comptes et griffonne sur son cahier des indications pour le
40 lendemain. Avant de partir, elle jette un dernier coup d'œil sur la liste des départs et des réservations. Demain, il faudra commencer son travail à 7 heures.

[1] les habitués: the regulars
[2] revenir sur: to go back over
[3] un commis: an assistant
[4] les prestations: service

Questions

1. In paragraph 1 we are told how Annie spends the first part of her day.

    (a) What is the very first thing she does?   **2 points**

    (b) What does she discuss with her regulars?   **1 point**

    (c) Why does she then go to reception?   **1 point**

2. The bedrooms have to be seen to (lines 7–10).

    (a) What does she go over with the chambermaids?   **3 points**

    (b) Mention three things which could spoil the hotel's image.   **3 points**

3. Read paragraph 3.

    (a) What does Annie discuss with the chef?   **2 points**

    (b) Apart from fellow hoteliers, who does Annie meet up with when she goes to the market?   **1 point**

4. Annie also has administrative work to do (lines 22–26).

    (a) What exactly keeps her busy in her office?   **2 points**

    (b) What determines how much money she makes daily?   **1 point**

5. Annie sorts out her business with her accountant (lines 27–32).

    (a) What does she need to renegotiate?   **1 point**

    (b) Why is it important for her to invest in the business?   **2 points**

6. Annie continues to work into the evening (lines 33–41).
   What is the last thing she does before leaving?   **1 point**

   (20 points)

   = 20 marks

7. Translate into English:

   "une dizaine . . . le tour des tables." (lines 18–20)   **10**

   (30)

Passage 8

Read the article carefully, then answer **in English** the questions which follow it.
You may use a French dictionary.

This article is about the advantages and disadvantages of working part-time.

Je travaille sur quatre jours

Martine, 33 ans

Mariée, Martine ne travaille ni le mercredi ni le vendredi. Ses deux enfants, Mathilde et
Victor, ont 4 ans et demi et 3 ans. «C'est la naissance de ma fille qui a provoqué l'envie de
temps partiel. A 29 ans, j'ai eu un bébé très souhaité. J'ai préféré avoir du temps à moi pour
5   m'en occuper. Quand j'en ai parlé à mon mari pour la première fois, il m'a dit: pourquoi
pas? Il n'y a eu aucun conflit. Je me sens plus calme en travaillant comme ça.»

Véronique, 33 ans

Célibataire et sans enfant, Véronique travaille depuis quinze ans dans une société privée.
Elle ne travaille pas le vendredi. «Je n'avais jamais de temps. Tout allait trop vite. Pendant
10 la semaine, je ne voyais personne, je ne faisais rien. Le week-end était trop court et je ne
pouvais aller nulle part. Maintenant, le vendredi, je peux faire les courses et aller chez le
coiffeur. Je fais les choses plus tranquillement. Le week-end je peux aussi m'entraîner à
l'escalade, faire du footing, aller à la piscine. J'ai aussi la possibilité de partir en montagne
pendant trois jours. J'ai perdu 20% de mon salaire, mais comme je n'ai personne à charge,
15 ça va.»

Hugues, 41 ans

Ouvrier, il ne travaille que quatre jours par semaine depuis le 1er juillet dernier. Ce n'est
pas un choix mais une décision de l'entreprise. Il a perdu 1300 francs de salaire mensuel et
gagné tous ses jeudis. «Je profite de ce temps pour faire des travaux dans la maison: la salle
20 de jeu des enfants, les clôtures. Dans trois ou quatre ans, peut-être que je travaillerai à
nouveau à temps complet. Quand je n'aurai plus rien à faire dans la maison. Sinon, il
faudrait que je trouve un autre loisir: rien ne m'attire. Je ne pêche pas, je ne chasse pas non
plus. Je ne lis pas beaucoup. Le dimanche, on se promène. On va à la mer, mais je ne sais
pas nager. Au printemps prochain, je ferai le jardin autour de la maison. Je mettrai des
25 tomates et des pommes de terre. Le jeudi, à leur retour de l'école, c'est moi qui fais faire les
devoirs aux enfants. L'argent? Nous n'avons pas changé notre façon de vivre. On fait
moins d'économies, c'est tout.»

Bernard, 40 ans

30   Il est médecin de campagne quatre jours par semaine. Marié, il consacre le mercredi à ses quatre enfants. «Je me suis organisé pour travailler quatre jours par semaine. Ma femme ne peut pas s'occuper des enfants le mercredi car elle travaille le mercredi: elle est éducatrice[1]. C'est moi qui m'en occupe. Quand on habite à la campagne, pour que les enfants puissent avoir des activités, il faut passer beaucoup de temps sur la route. Mais c'est un choix. Comme ils ont des âges différents, ils ne vont pas toujours à l'école en
35   même temps. Donc il faut s'adapter. Cette année, aucun d'entre eux n'a classe le samedi matin. Cela va nous permettre de partir en week-end dès le vendredi soir. Je suis aussi président d'une association[2] culturelle et je joue du piano toutes les semaines, du blues, du jazz, un peu de tout. Deux fois par mois, nous donnons des concerts dans le cadre de l'association. La vie associative est très importante pour moi.»

[1] une éducatrice: a teacher in a special school
[2] une association: a club

Questions

1. Martine decided to work part-time.

    (a) What prompted this decision?   **2 points**

    (b) How did her husband respond to her working part-time?   **2 points**

2. Véronique tells us what life used to be like before she worked a 4-day week.

    (a) How was her working week?   **3 points**

    (b) What can she do now on a Friday?   **2 points**

    (c) Mention two things she can now do at the weekend.   **2 points**

    (d) Her salary has been cut. Why does she not see this as a problem? **1 point**

3. Hugues mentions his circumstances.

    (a) Why does he work a 4-day week?   **1 point**

    (b) What does he do with his extra time?   **2 points**

    (c) Hugues' family lifestyle has not changed. He mentions one difference. What
         is it?   **1 point**

4. Bernard lives in the country.

    (a) So that his children can take part in different activities, what does he have to
         do?   **1 point**

    (b) As none of his children has school on Saturday morning, what will this allow
         the family to do?   **1 point**

    (c) Mention two things Bernard does at his club.   **2 points**

                                                                        (20 points)

                                                                        = 20 marks

5. Translate into English:

    "Je ne pêche pas . . . pommes de terre." (lines 22–25)   **10**

                                                                           (30)

Passage 9

Read the article carefully, then answer **in English** the questions which follow it.
You may use a French dictionary.

This article is about three young people who are determined to live their dreams.

Les ambitions des jeunes

Nathalie, une grande fille blonde de vingt-six ans, est en train d'entraîner son cheval. Son objectif: la sélection pour les prochains championnats de France. Elle doit travailler plus que les autres. Ils verront les difficultés. Pas elle. Nathalie est pratiquement aveugle. Elle ne distingue que des ombres[1].

5 Nathalie n'a jamais pensé à renoncer[2]. Elle se décrit elle-même comme "impulsive"; c'est le nom qu'elle donne à son incroyable ténacité. «Quand j'étais petite, je n'étais pas comme d'autres jeunes filles, je ne jouais pas avec des poupées mais avec des chevaux ou des fermes miniatures.»

Elle se souvient encore du souffle des chevaux qui venaient paître[3] derrière la maison
10 familiale, de la joie de ses premières promenades à dos de poney. Rien ne l'arrêtera. Ni les moyens modestes de ses parents, tous deux ouvriers, ni la rebuffade[4] d'un premier entraîneur qui croit qu'elle "n'y arrivera pas".

«J'ai toujours voulu être la meilleure . . . » Elle tient parole, s'entraîne intensivement, et saute des obstacles en les devinant. Avec Kofu, son premier cheval, elle remporte deux fois
15 les championnats de France. Il y a quelques années, elle échoue de peu à la sélection des championnats du monde. Elle la retentera . . .

Dans sa vie professionnelle aussi, Nathalie est toujours optimiste. Elle quitte une école spécialisée pour suivre toutes ses études secondaires dans un lycée normal, à l'aide d'une machine à écrire en braille et de cassettes. Elle étudie italien et espagnol, à l'université de
20 Paris, prenant chaque jour le train de Calais. Après une première expérience professionnelle, elle est sur le point d'être recrutée à un poste commercial par une grande société nationale. Elle veut être la meilleure.

Sophie voulait travailler dans l'aviation en Grande-Bretagne "pour aller voir ailleurs". Presque impossible à première vue, quand on est femme et Française, dans un milieu où
25 99% des employés sont des hommes et des Anglais. Mais Sophie, vingt-quatre ans, veut absolument y aller. Juste après son diplôme d'ingénieur, elle envoie des lettres de

candidature[5]. Trois mois après, elle travaille près de Londres dans une grande compagnie de l'aéronautique. Sur une centaine de cadres employés par cette entreprise, <u>il y a seulement quatre femmes, et une seule Française: Sophie.</u>

30 <u>Ses collègues britanniques, un peu froids au début, l'adoptent rapidement, même comme partenaire de golf le dimanche.</u> Mais elle ne fait que commencer: «Plus tard, je voudrais aller travailler au Canada ou en Australie, des pays qui me font rêver.» Et quand Sophie a décidé quelque chose . . .

Toussaint Roze a dix-sept ans, ce qui étonnerait bien les centaines de personnes qui ont
35 acheté son logiciel de généalogie[6], *Win Genealogic*. Un système qui permet de dessiner des arbres généalogiques, et de produire des statistiques sur les aïeux.

Il consacre toutes les journées de ses grandes vacances à son logiciel. A la rentrée, il offre gratuitement ses disquettes à une vingtaine de distributeurs, qui les vendent 30F.

Les projets de Toussaint? Sortir bientôt une version améliorée de son logiciel. Il est aussi
40 en train de . . . redoubler sa terminale au lycée. «Je n'avais pas le temps d'étudier» avoue-t-il. Veut-il fonder plus tard une vraie société d'informatique? «Pas forcément. J'ai plein d'autres idées. Je suis très créatif.» On n'en doute pas . . .

[1] une ombre: a shadow
[2] renoncer: to give up
[3] paître: to graze
[4] une rebuffade: a rebuff
[5] une lettre de candidature: application form
[6] un logiciel de généalogie: computer software on ancestry

Questions

1. Nathalie has to work harder than others in training for the French horse-riding championships.
    Why is this?   **2 points**

2. Nathalie was unlike most other little girls.
    How do you know this?   **2 points**

3. Two things might have put her off training professionally (lines 9–12).
    Mention two obstacles.   **3 points**

4. Nathalie trains intensively.
    How does she manage the jumps?   **1 point**

5. Read paragraph 5.
    Nathalie leaves a special school to study in mainstream education.

    (a) What help is she given in school?   **2 points**

    (b) What evidence is there that she is successful at this school?   **1 point**

6. Sophie is determined to work in the aeronautics industry in Britain (lines 23–33).

    (a) Why does the author consider this to be practically impossible?   **3 points**

    (b) Her ambition does not stop there. What are her future plans?   **1 point**

7. Toussaint is a successful producer of computer software (lines 34–42).

    (a) What would surprise a lot of people about him?   **1 point**

    (b) What does his software allow you to do?   **2 points**

    (c) What are his future plans?   **1 point**

    (d) Why is he having to repeat a school year?   **1 point**

                                                                                        (20 points)

                                                                                        = 20 marks

8. Translate into English:

    "il y a seulement . . . fait que commencer". (lines 28–31)   **10**
                                                                                        (30)

Passage 10

Read the article carefully, then answer **in English** the questions which follow it.
You may use a French dictionary.

This article is about a day in the life of a teacher who works in a deprived area of Paris.

Prof de banlieue

Sept heures trente. J'arrive. Je me suis levée à six heures. Le lit était chaud et dehors il faisait froid. J'ai pris le métro, changé Place-de-Clichy, repris un métro et, à la sortie du métro, encore un bus. Puis j'ai fini le trajet à pied: une heure. Le collège est vide. Le soleil se lève.

5   Je suis prof de banlieue. Le lundi matin est affreux. Lundi matin, et toute la semaine qui vient, pleine d'élèves qui crient, de copies[1] à corriger, de migraines. En vérité, je ne suis pas prof de banlieue, mais professeur d'anglais. «Hello, teacher!» disent mes élèves quand ils me voient. Ils gribouillent sur le tableau en passant, tripotent le magnétophone, me caressent les cheveux: «Ils sont doux! Vous venez de faire un shampooing?» Ils jettent
10 leurs sacs sur les tables, s'assoient enfin, sortent leurs livres d'anglais. Le cours peut commencer.

Il est 8 heures 25 lorsque Mohand (surnommé[2] Gros Porc) émet un cri de cochon. J'étais en train d'expliquer, avec la concentration nécessaire, un point de grammaire, et tout le monde écoutait attentivement. Sauf Mohand. Je me suis fâchée. Il a marmonné: «Espèce
15 de *****!» dans un silence qui l'a surpris lui-même, et tous l'ont entendu . . . moi aussi, et je me suis sentie blêmir de la tête aux pieds. «Fort bien! Je fais un rapport disciplinaire.» Ils ont frémi.

A la récréation de 10 heures, je remets ce rapport au secrétariat. A 10 heures 32, le principal est entré dans ma salle, l'air furieux. Tous les élèves sont debout, impressionnés. Mohand a
20 été sommé de venir devant moi et de s'excuser. Il a bredouillé[3]: «Je m'excuse.» «Non, monsieur! a tonné le directeur, on ne s'excuse pas! On dit: "Je vous prie de bien vouloir accepter mes excuses, Madame." Répète!» Il a répété, les yeux baissés, penaud[4], et j'ai répondu: «Je les accepte», après avoir longuement réfléchi. Le principal a rappelé fermement les règles de base du collège: respect des professeurs et des camarades et il faut
25 travailler dur. Sur quoi, il est sorti et chacun s'est remis[5] à respirer. J'ai répété que l'école est une chance pour eux, enfants d'immigrés, de chômeurs, et de familles modestes. Chance à ne pas laisser passer! Mohand avait la "honte" et la "haine", m'assassinait de ses grands yeux noirs. A la sonnerie de 11 heures 30, il m'a donné un papier: «En fait, je vous aime bien. Votre élève, Mohand.»

30 A 11 heures 33, Gladys a annoncé: «Il y a le feu dans le couloir, Madame!» «Pas de panique, ai-je répondu, tout le monde sort! Allez vite, vite, vite!» Ils ont descendu les deux étages en hurlant. «Ne hurlez pas!» hurlais-je. Une poubelle flambait dans le couloir, la fumée nous étouffait. «Ce n'est rien, ce n'est pas grave, a dit le principal. Maintenant, vous pouvez remonter.» Dans la salle de classe je les ai fait taire et ai affirmé qu'on trouverait

35 l'incendiaire[6], et qu'il serait sévèrement puni. J'ai menti, on ne le trouvera pas.

Dans l'après-midi un peu de solennité: contrôle d'anglais. Les élèves prennent le contrôle au sérieux car c'est difficile. Assise à mon bureau je les regarde travailler. Ils ne rient plus. Je les aime bien. Ils sont travailleurs et enthousiastes. Ils rêvent d'un beau métier. Je leur dis: «Courage, travaillez!» C'est tout ce que je peux faire pour eux. Ça et un peu d'anglais.

40 Ça sonne. «Rendez vos copies! . . . » Ô joie, la journée est finie! Je range mes affaires. En sortant ils crient: «Good bye, teacher! A demain!»

[1] une copie: written work
[2] surnommé: nicknamed
[3] bredouiller: to stammer
[4] penaud: sheepishly
[5] se remettre: to begin again
[6] l'incendiaire: arsonist

36

Questions

1. The teacher does not like Mondays. Why not?   **2 points**

2. When her pupils come into the classroom they appear quite unruly (lines 7–11).
    Mention three things they do before sitting down.   **3 points**

3. Read paragraph 3.

    (a) In what way does Mohand interrupt the lesson?   **1 point**

    (b) Why is the teacher particularly annoyed with this interruption?   **2 points**

    (c) What action does she take when he swears at her?   **1 point**

4. The headmaster comes into the classroom (lines 18–29).

    (a) How does he punish Mohand?   **2 points**

    (b) The headmaster reminds the class of the basic school rules. What are they?   **2 points**

    (c) What sort of background do these pupils come from?   **3 points**

    (d) What touching gesture does Mohand make towards his teacher at the end of the lesson?   **2 points**

5. The lesson is interrupted again (lines 30–35).
    Why do the pupils have to leave the classroom at 11.33?   **1 point**

6. In the final paragraph we are told of the pupils' dreams.
    What do they hope for?   **1 point**

                                                                                                      (20 points)

                                                                                                      = 20 marks

7. Translate into English:

    "Les élèves prennent . . . et enthousiastes." (lines 36–38)   **10**
                                                                                                      (30)

Passage 11

Read the article carefully, then answer **in English** the questions which follow it.
You may use a French dictionary.

This article is about French people who work in London.

Vivre à Londres

Christophe Pénelon, 31 ans, est chauffeur de bus. Banal? Non. Son bus est un *double-decker* rouge qui roule à gauche. Car c'est dans les rues de Londres que Christophe exerce son métier. Son aventure a commencé dans une agence nationale pour l'emploi à Marseille où il a aperçu une petite annonce: «Compagnie de bus londoniens cherche conducteurs
5 français.» Il avait envie d'une expérience nouvelle, d'apprendre l'anglais, et surtout de conduire l'un de ces bus à impériale. Après trois semaines de formation à Londres et un cours intensif d'anglais maintenant il travaille dans les rues de la capitale. Pour un salaire d'environ 250 livres par semaine, Christophe est ravi. Son seul problème: comprendre les questions des passagers, dont l'accent n'est pas toujours celui d'Oxford!

10 Mais les Français ne travaillent pas que dans les bus. <u>«Ici à Londres, les Français sont partout. Ils travaillent dans les restaurants et les boîtes de nuit, ainsi que dans les banques et les compagnies d'assurances, sans oublier les équipes de football et même l'industrie du cinéma!»</u> Hélène Verdier connaît Londres comme sa poche. Cette femme est l'une des costumières[1] les plus demandées par la télévision et le cinéma. «Même dans mon domaine,
15 où les Français étaient rares parce qu'ils ne maîtrisaient pas la langue, ils deviennent de plus en plus nombreux.»

Sur les 300 000 Français installés en Grande-Bretagne, plus de 180 000 se sont établis dans la capitale. Parmi eux figurent des jeunes qui arrivent en grand nombre, la plupart du temps pour une période assez courte, allant de trois mois à deux ans. 80% viennent pour travailler
20 dans les restaurants ou les hôtels.

Il y a les autres aussi, ceux qui, souvent, ont quitté une vie confortable et qui viennent à Londres dans l'espoir de tenter autre chose, autrement. Pour François Raffenaud l'aventure a commencé il y a seulement deux ans. Acteur de théâtre dans une troupe parisienne, il avait devant lui une carrière prometteuse et menait une vie réussie: un salaire confortable,
25 un bel appartement et beaucoup de propositions de rôles. «Je m'ennuyais à Paris et j'avais besoin d'aller vivre ailleurs. Je suis d'abord venu à Londres pour une semaine. Je l'ai tout de suite aimé et je suis resté. Aujourd'hui j'ai le sentiment profond d'avoir fait le bon choix.» Quand il n'est pas au théâtre, François gagne un peu plus en devenant le baby-sitter de plusieurs familles aisées[2].

30 Olivier Fleurot est directeur du quotidien *Financial Times*. Il est en effet le premier
Français à diriger le journal. «Pour les Anglais, un bon employé n'est pas forcément celui
qui reste tard pour finir des dossiers, explique-t-il, le travail est intensif, les pauses déjeuner
sont courtes et, à 17h30, on rentre à la maison. L'employé qui reste plus tard n'est pas bien
considéré. Il sera vu comme celui qui n'a pas su organiser sa journée.»

35 Si Londres offre de multiples possibilités de travail, la vie londonienne coûte extrêmement
cher, surtout le logement. Les étudiants et les célibataires peuvent se débrouiller[3] en
choisissant la solution de la colocation[4]. Mais pour une famille le choix est souvent
déterminé par la proximité du lycée français, situé dans le quartier chic de Kensington, où
les loyers sont exorbitants.

40 Gilles Thieffry, avocat, a préféré acheter. «Aujourd'hui, je ne pourrais plus acheter la
maison que j'ai acquise il y a dix ans.» Une autre grande dépense pour une famille, ce sont
les frais de scolarité. «Pour mon fils, qui va au lycée français, cela revient à 7 500F par
trimestre. J'ai vécu des années aux États-Unis avant de venir à Londres et, croyez-moi, la
vie est bien plus chère ici.»

45 A Londres, tout n'est pas si simple. Si on veut habiter Londres, on peut, d'accord, mais il
faut en payer le prix . . .

[1] une costumière: costume designer
[2] aisé: well-off
[3] se débrouiller: to get by
[4] la colocation: shared tenancy

Questions

1. Christophe is now working in London.

    (a) How did he find out about his current job? **2 points**

    (b) Why was he attracted to the post? **3 points**

    (c) What is the only problem in his new job? **2 points**

2. In the second paragraph Hélène Verdier, another expatriate living in London, suggests why there used to be so few French people working for British cinema and television.
   What reason does she give? **1 point**

3. Read paragraph 3.
   What are we told about the 180 000+ young French people who come to work in London? **3 points**

4. François is an actor from Paris.

    (a) How do you know that he had a successful lifestyle and career? **2 points**

    (b) How does he earn extra cash in London? **2 points**

5. Read lines 30 to 34.
   According to Olivier, why is an employee who works late not highly regarded in Britain? **1 point**

6. In paragraph 6 we are told of the disadvantages of living in London.

    (a) What might determine where a French family lives? **1 point**

    (b) Why might living in Kensington be out of the question? **1 point**

7. Gilles preferred to buy his London home rather than rent.
   What other considerable family expense does he mention? **1 point**

8. What conclusion does the author draw in her final comment? **1 point**

    (20 points)

    = 20 marks

9. Translate into English:
   "Ici à Londres . . . cinéma!" (lines 10–13) **10**

    (30)

THE WIDER WORLD

Passage 12

Read the article carefully, then answer **in English** the questions which follow it.
You may use a French dictionary.

This article is about life in South Korea and how things have changed for one family in the last 50 years.

Je gagne plus en un mois que mon père en un an

«Parfois, quand je me promène dans Séoul, je ne reconnais plus mon pays» dit Lee Sung-Hee, une vieille dame de 72 ans. C'est vrai, tout a changé en Corée du Sud. Pays agricole au début des années 60, elle est devenue aujourd'hui la onzième puissance industrielle du globe.

5 «Je suis née à Noktong, un petit village de pêcheurs. Notre maison, d'une seule pièce, avait un toit de chaume. A cette époque, la Corée était occupée par le Japon. Je n'avais que deux habits quand j'étais petite. On n'avait pas d'argent, mais je n'ai jamais eu faim, à la différence de ceux qui habitaient en ville. Dans une famille de pêcheurs, il y a toujours du poisson. Comme j'étais une jeune fille, je ne suis pas allée à l'école. Je n'étais jamais
10 malheureuse, je ne connaissais que cette vie.»

Park Chon-Soo, son fils, naît en 1952, pendant la guerre[1] entre le Nord et le Sud de la Corée. Lorsque le conflit prend fin en 1953, la Corée du Sud est ruinée. La famine sévit. Le pays ne survit que grâce à l'aide internationale.

La chance de Park Chon-Soo viendra de l'éducation. Le gouvernement adopte un plan de
15 scolarisation massive, car 75% de la population est analphabète. Park Chon-Soo entre au collège en 1964. Il est le premier de sa famille à aller "si loin" dans les études. Mais à 16 ans, on lui barre l'accès au lycée à cause de ses origines sociales. «Les fils d'ouvriers ou de paysans n'avaient pas le droit d'aller à l'université.» Il apprendra la mécanique. Car la Corée est une nation-entreprise. Sous couvert de[2] libéralisme, le gouvernement décide
20 tout. C'est le "capitalisme d'État".

La population obéit par nationalisme et par crainte de la répression. En outre[3], l'influence de Confucius, un penseur chinois du VIe siècle avant Jésus-Christ, est encore dominante dans la société coréenne. L'école de pensée confucianiste insiste sur le respect du travail, le désir d'éducation, la solidarité familiale et la loyauté envers le pays.

25 En 1972, Park Chon-Soo est embauché[4] chez Hyundai, la plus grosse firme du pays. En 1973, il se marie et son fils, Park Soo-Kyong, naît en 1975. Son père garde un souvenir mitigé des années 70: «On ne faisait que travailler, dix heures par jour, six jours par semaine. Les inégalités sociales étaient criantes, mais nos salaires augmentaient vite. Je gagnais plus en un mois que mon père en un an autrefois.» La première fois qu'il a pris
30 conscience de son enrichissement? «Quand j'ai pu acheter du papier toilette, répond-il gêné. Dépenser de l'argent pour ça, c'était un tel changement!»

Aujourd'hui, les Park gagnent environ 20 000F par mois. Leur logement dispose de l'électronique dernier cri[5]. Park Soo-Kyong écoute son père et sa grand-mère en souriant. Lui, il préfère la mode, et les chanteurs. En étant admis dans une faculté de mathématiques,
35 Park Soo-Kyong a vengé son père. Mais il ne se fait pas d'illusion. Après ses deux ans et demi de service militaire, il espère bien être embauché dans une grande entreprise. Et il sait qu'alors, lui aussi entrera dans le moule coréen.

[1] la guerre: war
[2] sous couvert de: under cover of
[3] en outre: moreover
[4] embaucher: to take on
[5] dernier cri: the latest

Questions

1. Lee Sung-Hee no longer recognises Seoul.
    What change has she seen in the last 40 years? **2 points**

2. She mentions what life used to be like (lines 5–10).

    (a) How does she describe her house? **2 points**

    (b) Why was it fortunate that her family were fishermen? **1 point**

    (c) Why was she never unhappy? **1 point**

3. We are told about her son, Park Chon-Soo (lines 11–20).

    (a) What was South Korea like just after he was born? **2 points**

    (b) Why did the country embark on a massive education programme? **1 point**

    (c) Why was Park Chon-Soo forbidden access to higher education? **2 points**

4. We are told about Confucius' influence (lines 21–24).

    (a) Who exactly was he? **2 points**

    (b) What is his school of thought? **3 points**

5. For many people working conditions improved in 70s Korea (lines 25–31).

    (a) In what way was Park Chon-Soo better off than his father had been? **1 point**

    (b) When did he first become aware of his prosperity? **1 point**

6. In the final paragraph we are told what things are like today for the Park family.

    (a) What is Park Soo-Kyong now interested in? **1 point**

    (b) In what way has he had more opportunities than his father? **1 point**

    (20 points)

    = 20 marks

7. Translate into English:

    "A cette époche . . . habitaient en ville." (lines 6–8). **10**

    (30)

Passage 13

Read the article carefully, then answer **in English** the questions which follow it.
You may use a French dictionary.

This article is about the lives of young people in three Chinese cities: Peking, Xian and Shanghai, fifty years after the rise in communism.

La nouvelle Chine

Kim est secrétaire et travaille depuis six mois dans une petite société d'informatique de Pékin. «Je sors au moins une fois par semaine en boîte de nuit, au cinéma ou au karaoké avec des copains et des copines», explique-t-elle.

Issue d'[1] une famille modeste d'ouvriers, Kim est fille unique, née en 1979, un an après
5   l'application de la «loi de l'enfant unique» interdisant aux couples chinois d'avoir plus d'un enfant. Elle est entrée dans le monde du travail à la sortie du lycée. «Je voulais gagner mon argent très vite. J'habite toujours chez mes parents, je les aide financièrement. Je travaille beaucoup mais j'arrive à[2] gagner plus de 1500 yuans (1000F) par mois. Je prends des cours du soir pour apprendre l'informatique, et un jour, je monterai ma propre
10 entreprise.»

La Chine dans laquelle Kim et toute sa génération vivent n'a jamais été aussi prospère. Au cœur de Pékin il y a des embouteillages: les traditionnelles bicyclettes de la capitale partagent les rues avec des milliers de taxis, Mercedes et BMW. Les grandes cités chinoises qui s'endormaient à 18h30 il y a vingt ans, s'illuminent aujourd'hui des mille
15 feux des centres commerciaux ouverts tard le soir, des restaurants branchés[3], des discothèques . . .

Les Chinois aiment acheter. Dans leurs appartements tout neufs, les nouveaux propriétaires possèdent tous une télévision (une deuxième pour l'enfant unique), un magnétoscope (ou plus souvent un lecteur DVD), un réfrigérateur-congélateur, une machine à laver et un
20 canapé de cuir.

Étudiante à l'université de Xian, Wu Lan, 20 ans, elle aussi fille unique, reconnaît qu'elle appartient à une génération chanceuse. «Par rapport à mes parents qui ont travaillé toute leur vie pour un salaire minable, sans aucun loisir ni aucune liberté, je suis consciente d'être très privilégiée. Mes parents ont été très sévères avec moi et me disputaient souvent,
25 peut-être parce que ma mère, institutrice, savait ce qui était bon ou mauvais pour moi.»

Alors que ses parents ont eu un mariage arrangé, Wu a choisi son petit copain. «Ce n'est plus tabou de se promener dans la rue main dans la main et même de s'embrasser dans un parc», raconte-t-elle. Alors qu'une telle chose était totalement prohibée[4] il n'y a pas si longtemps.

30 Wu n'est apparement pas intéressée par l'argent. Elle veut devenir professeur, ce qui veut dire rester «pauvre» puisqu'un professeur ne gagne pas plus de 500 yuans par mois. En plus, elle s'accorde avec la politique de l'enfant unique du gouvernement: «Nous sommes trop nombreux en Chine.»

Comme toute la jeunesse shanghaienne, quand il veut s'amuser, Chang Yie ira au bowling 35 ou au cybercafé. Une vingtaine d'ordinateurs sont alignés là et le soir beaucoup de jeunes surfent sur le Web. Avec sa copine, Chang Yie y va trois fois par semaine: «On s'amuse beaucoup, raconte-t-il. On peut tout faire avec ça, c'est une nouvelle vision du monde: chercher un job, consulter les annonces pour acheter une voiture ou un appartement, envoyer des messages à des amis à l'étranger, dialoguer en direct sur tous les sujets 40 possibles . . .»

Personne ne se pose la question de savoir ce qui est autorisé ou pas dans un régime toujours officiellement communiste où les médias sont sévèrement contrôlés et les opposants facilement jetés en prison. Les sites des universités australiennes ou américaines qui présentent leurs conditions d'entrée sont aussi appréciés par les surfeurs. En les consultant, 45 Chang Yie n'a pas l'impression de transgresser[5] la loi: «Si ce cybercafé existe, c'est que je peux m'en servir pour mes projets personnels.» La vie est aussi simple que cela . . .

[1] issu de: born of
[2] arriver à: to manage to
[3] branché: trendy
[4] prohibé: forbidden
[5] transgresser: to break

Questions

1. Kim is one of the new Chinese generation.
    Where has she been working for the last six months?   **1 point**

2. In the second paragraph we are told something about recent Chinese history.

    (a) What exactly is the "loi de l'enfant unique"?   **3 points**

    (b) What does Kim do in the evening?   **1 point**

    (c) What does she hope to do one day?   **1 point**

3. There are drawbacks to the booming Chinese economy.
    What is the problem in Peking city centre today?   **1 point**

4. Twenty years ago nothing much would happen in Chinese cities after 6.30pm.
    How have things changed?   **2 points**

5. Wu Lan realises that her generation is lucky compared to her parents'
    (lines 21–25).

    (a) Why does she feel so fortunate?   **3 points**

    (b) What did her mother work as?   **1 point**

6. Wu Lan has a boyfriend. In China showing affection in public is no longer taboo.
    How are Wu Lan and her boyfriend able to show their feelings for each other?   **2 points**

7. We are told about young people in Shanghai (lines 34–46).

    (a) Where does Chang Yie go to have fun?   **2 points**

    (b) Mention two things Chang Yie and his girlfriend might do on the net.   **2 points**

    (c) Why are the Australian and American university websites appreciated by
          Chinese internet surfers?   **1 point**

                                                                                        (20 points)

                                                                                        = 20 marks

8. Translate into English:

    "Les Chinois aiment . . . de cuir." (lines 17–20).   **10**

                                                                                            (30)

Passage 14

Read the article carefully, then answer **in English** the questions which follow it.
You may use a French dictionary.

This article is about a French couple who set off on a trip around the world.

Le tour du monde à vélo

Une idée un peu folle

<u>Lyon 1978</u>: Claude, technicien de 25 ans, et Françoise, étudiante en décoration intérieure
de 21 ans, veulent découvrir le monde et se faire de nouveaux amis. Mais comment? Ils
envisagent plusieurs possibilités: voyager à moto, à pied. Mais la moto est trop chère et la
5   marche à pied est trop lente. Finalement ils trouvent la solution: le vélo leur offre un moyen
économique, indépendant et pratique de se déplacer. C'est un moyen de transport non-
agressif qui attire la curiosité des gens. Cependant, il y a un petit problème: Claude et
Françoise n'ont jamais fait de vélo! Une longue préparation de deux ans commence:
trouver les bons vélos, économiser de l'argent, préparer l'itinéraire, se renseigner sur les
10 différentes destinations, faire des vaccinations et apprendre l'anglais.

Le départ

<u>Lyon, 1er avril 1980</u>: Claude et Françoise sont prêts. Ils ont leurs vélos faits sur mesure[1],
80 000 francs en poche (toutes leurs économies) et surtout un désir de vivre une grande
aventure. Ils ne veulent pas battre de records. Non, ils veulent rencontrer les habitants de la
15 Terre et voir le monde.

Journal de voyage

<u>Népal, décembre 81</u>: Claude et Françoise passent le réveillon de Noël à Kathmandou. Ils
ont été invités dans une maison habitée par un couple et une cinquantaine d'orphelins. La
"famille" va célébrer Noël. Mais quelle surprise lorsque Claude et Françoise voient arriver
20 le Père Noël sur un éléphant!

<u>Thaïlande, janvier 82</u>: Ils roulent tranquillement sur une petite route dans le sud du pays.
Soudain, deux jeunes à moto les menacent avec des revolvers. Ils sont seuls sur cette route.
Heureusement, quelques minutes plus tard, des camions arrivent. Les bandits fuient à
moto!

25   Australie, décembre 87: Françoise tombe enceinte[2]. Cette grossesse[3] n'empêche pas la suite de l'aventure. Après l'Australie, c'est la Nouvelle-Zélande où Manon naîtra le 12 septembre 1988. Cette naissance ne changera rien au voyage. Une remorque sera attachée au vélo de Françoise et il faudra transporter quelques sacs supplémentaires!

Canada, juillet 90: La circulation au Canada et aux États-Unis est intense. Les voitures sont
30   partout et les risques d'accidents sont élevés. Solution au problème? Deux Canadiens, devenus amis, la trouvent. Ils ont commandé deux voitures de police pour escorter Claude et Françoise à Montréal.

France, avril 1994: La famille Hervé retrouve le sol français. Derniers coups de pédales en direction de Paris où les attendent famille et amis.

35   *Une grande récompense*

Lorsque des amis ou des curieux demandent à Claude et Françoise ce qui leur a fait le plus peur, ils s'attendent à des réponses comme les maladies, les animaux dangereux et les vols. Ils ont tort. C'est la route. La circulation frénétique des pays asiatiques, les petites routes enneigées de l'Himalaya, les pistes innondées des forêts d'Amérique du Sud, le sable des
40   déserts africains, la vitesse sur les routes d'Amérique du Nord sont les vrais dangers. Chaque jour, pendant quatorze ans, les Hervé ont risqué leur vie. Mais ça en valait la peine[4]. Cette grande aventure a permis à la famille Hervé d'apprendre à tolérer, à accepter sans juger et à prendre le temps d'observer le monde. De retour en France, Claude, Françoise et Manon veulent maintenant vivre en toute simplicité.

[1] fait sur mesure: made-to-measure
[2] enceinte: pregnant
[3] la grossesse: pregnancy
[4] valoir la peine: to be worth it

Questions

1. Claude and Françoise have the crazy idea of going round the world on a bike.

   (a) Why do they dismiss the idea of travelling by motorbike or on foot?   **2 points**

   (b) What slight problem do they foresee?   **1 point**

   (c) Mention three things they have to do in preparation for their journey.   **3 points**

2. Claude and Françoise go to Nepal.

   (a) With whom do they spend Christmas Eve?   **2 points**

   (b) What surprise is in store for them?   **2 points**

3. Their adventure continues in Thailand.

   (a) What happens to them in the south of the country?   **2 points**

   (b) How is the situation resolved?   **2 points**

4. In Australia Françoise gets pregnant. How does this affect their journey?   **3 points**

5. In the final paragraph we are told why Claude and Françoise feel the trip was worth it. Give three reasons.   **3 points**

   (20 points)

   = 20 marks

6. Translate into English:

   "Lorsque des amis . . . Ils ont tort." (lines 36–38).   **10**

   (30)

Passage 15

Read the article carefully, then answer **in English** the questions which follow it.
You may use a French dictionary.

This article is about starving children in the world today.

Manger à sa faim

Pema est impatient: il est plus de midi. Il a 12 ans et une faim de loup[1]. Sa mère lui sert un mélange de riz et de pommes de terre et il avale tout avec appétit. Déjà, Pema a mangé la même chose hier et tous les autres jours de la semaine. Patates et riz, voilà l'unique menu de sa famille depuis bien longtemps. Midi et soir.

5· Car la famille de Pema est très pauvre. D'origine tibétaine, Pema, ses parents, son frère et ses deux sœurs ont été obligés de quitter leur pays et ils sont maintenant réfugiés en Inde. (La Chine occupe le Tibet et interdit aux Tibétains de vivre selon leurs traditions. Pour cette raison, de nombreux Tibétains vivent hors de leur pays.) Ils habitent une région où la terre n'est pas bonne. Le père de Pema cultive un peu de maïs, mais la dernière récolte a été
10 détruite par un cyclone . . .

Riz et pommes de terre seront donc encore au prochain menu. Pour leur donner un peu de goût, la mère de Pema y ajoute des piments[2]. La viande, c'est beaucoup trop cher: on n'en mange donc qu'une à deux fois par mois. Comme les légumes ou les fruits. Quelle fête quand papa rapporte des mangues!

15 Beaucoup d'amis de Pema sont malades parce qu'ils manquent de protéines et de vitamines. Tenzin, son meilleur copain, qui a 12 ans lui aussi, en paraît 8. Pema lui-même se trouve petit pour son âge. Pas facile de grandir quand on ne mange pas à sa faim!

Comme Pema et Tenzin, des millions d'enfants ne sont pas assez nourris. Or, une bonne nourriture est indispensable pour bien grandir et être en bonne santé. Certains enfants ne
20 mangent pas en quantité suffisante, ils sont sous-alimentés. D'autres n'ont pas une nourriture assez variée: ils souffrent de malnutrition. Le riz et les pommes de terre ne sont pas suffisants. Il faut manger aussi de la viande, des œufs, du poisson, des fruits et des légumes. La malnutrition provoque en effet de nombreuses maladies: maladies des yeux par manque de vitamine A et retard mental par manque d'iode[3]. Certaines de ces maladies
25 entraînent la mort. Dans le monde aujourd'hui, un enfant sur trois n'est pas assez nourri.

Pourtant, notre planète produit de quoi nourrir tous ses habitants. La faim n'est donc pas une question de quantité de nourriture, mais de partage. Les enfants qui ont faim vivent dans des pays, ou des familles, pauvres. La nourriture existe mais les parents n'ont pas d'argent pour en acheter. C'est le cas dans de nombreux pays d'Afrique et d'Asie.

30 Beaucoup d'enfants sont aussi victimes des guerres ou des conflits politiques. Leurs familles, comme celle de Pema, quittent leurs villages et se réfugient ailleurs. Les parents perdent leur travail ou la terre qu'ils cultivaient, et deviennent trop pauvres pour nourrir correctement leurs enfants.

Aujourd'hui, Pema est en vie, et en bonne santé, grâce à l'aide d'une association, 35 *Assistance médicale Toit du monde*, qui lui fournit les vitamines dont il a besoin pour bien grandir. Mais, comme tous les enfants du monde, Pema a un rêve: il espère qu'un jour, son père pourra travailler et gagner assez d'argent pour nourrir lui-même toute sa famille.

[1] avoir une faim de loup: to be ravenous
[2] des piments: peppers
[3] l'iode: iodine

Questions

1. Pema is very hungry.
    What is the staple diet in his family?   **2 points**

2. Pema and his family have had to leave their homeland (lines 5–10).

    (a) Why is this?   **3 points**

    (b) We are told that the soil in Pema's new homeland is not fertile. What other
           reason is given for the immediate shortage of food?   **1 point**

3. What are we told about meat in paragraph 3?   **2 points**

4. Many of Pema's friends are ill (lines 15–17).
    What alarming fact is revealed about Tenzin?   **1 point**

5. Read paragraph 5.
    We are told about the importance of good food.

    (a) Why is it essential?   **2 points**

    (b) According to the text what exactly is malnutrition?   **2 points**

    (c) Mention the two diseases caused by lack of vitamin A and iodine.   **2 points**

    (d) What statistic are we presented with at the end of this paragraph?   **1 point**

6. Our planet produces enough food for all of its inhabitants.
    Why are there still starving children in the world, especially in Africa and Asia?   **2 points**

7. Pema reveals his dream in the final paragraph.
    What is it?   **2 points**

                                                                                (20 points)

                                                                                = 20 marks

8. Translate into English:

    "Beaucoup d'enfants . . . leurs enfants." (lines 30–33).   **10**
                                                                                (30)

ANSWER SCHEMES

Passage 1

J'ai plongé à 17 ans

1. We are we told about the author's family background.

   (a) Mention two things.   **2 points**
   - his family was well-off (had no financial worries)
   - they lived in a nice part of Paris
   - his father was very authoritarian (strict)
     (any 2)

   (b) What two specific restrictions did his father impose on him as a child?   **2 points**
   - he was not allowed to go to play football with his friends
   - he could not bring his friends home

2. A major event happened in the author's life when he was 9.

   (a) What was it?   **1 point**
   - his best friend moved house

   (b) Why was this particularly traumatic for him?   **1 point**
   - he could not talk to anyone about it

3. The author started taking drugs (lines 12–16).

   (a) What reasons for this does he give?   **2 points**
   - he wanted to create a new family
   - he needed people he could talk to
   - he was attracted by the hippie lifestyle
     (any 2)

   (b) Why was his first experience not a happy one?   **2 points**
   - the drugs made him very ill
   - he had a splitting headache
   - he was very sick
     (any 2)

4. He went to university.
   What evidence is there that he was not interested in his studies?   **1 point**
   - he did not go regularly to lectures

5. He started going out with Nora (lines 25–29).
   After the birth of his child, why did he and Nora split up?   **3 points**
   - he thought it was possible to be a drug addict
   - and bring up a child at the same time
   - Nora did not agree

6.   The author met Patricia (lines 30–35).

   What happened one Christmas which finally prompted him to give up drugs for good?   **2 points**
   - his son had nothing to eat
   - all the money had gone on dope
   - he was so ashamed
      (any 2)

7.   The author has learned a lot from his experiences (lines 36–40).

   (a)   What is his plan for the future?   **2 points**
   - to rebuild a family
   - to bring up his son
   - to regain his son's trust
      (any 2)

   (b)   Why does he consider himself the best and worst role model for his son?
   - he is the worst for having fallen so low   **2 points**
   - he is the best for having come through it

   20 points

   = 20 marks

8.   Translate into English:

   "Une chose était . . . garder pour moi."   (lines 7–10)   **10**
   (30)

   ### Translation

   One thing was unbearable: we never talked,

   or   (rather)   we talked about trivial   things;
         (if we did)   insignificant
         (else)

   "Have you tidied (up) your room?" "What marks did you get in school today?"

                talked about   things
   We never discussed   serious matters. (We   never   had   a   serious
                                             conversation.)

   I suffered a lot in having to keep everything to myself.

Passage 2

Je ne supporte plus ma mère

1. In the first paragraph Florence mentions the change in her relationship with her mother.

    (a) What is it about her mother she cannot stand?   **2 points**
        - being in her presence
        - the sound of her voice
        - what she has to say
        (any 2)

    (b) If her mother had an argument with Florence's father or at work, how did Florence react?   **1 point**
        - she always thought her mother was right

2. Florence tells us about an incident she had with her mother recently (lines 8–15).

    (a) Why did her mother want her to come downstairs?   **2 points**
        - she wanted to speak to her
        - she had received a letter from her son
        - she wanted to read the letter to Florence
        (any 2)

    (b) How did Florence react upstairs to her mother's request?   **2 points**
        - she started to yell
        - covering her ears (putting her fingers in her ears)

    (c) What did her mother ask her when she came back home?   **1 point**
        - if she had calmed down

3. Florence used to be so proud of her mother.
    Why was this?   **2 points**
        - her school friends used to say how young, beautiful
        - and smartly dressed her mother was

4. In paragraph 4 Florence describes her mother's behaviour at home.

    (a) What is she like?   **3 points**
        - she presides (reigns) over everything and everyone
        - she is full of energy (dynamic)
        - she takes decisions
        - she talks a lot
        - she is the centre of attention
        (any 3)

    (b)   Mention two things on which her mother has an opinion.   **2 points**
- children's education
- teaching methods
- medicine
  (any 2)

5.   Florence compares her mother to her Aunt Madeleine (lines 25–29).
How do they differ?   **2 points**
- Aunt Madeleine does not speak much
- she is very attentive to her whole family and was towards Florence
- when you need her she is there for you
  (any 2)

6.   Florence mentions what it was like at first staying with her aunt (lines 30–34).
What was the one thing Florence learned about herself?   **2 points**
- all her ideas and thoughts were her mother's
- she expressed them with as much confidence as her mother

7.   From your reading of the final paragraph, how would you sum up the change in Florence's behaviour?   **1 point**
- she stands up to her mother

OR
- Florence is not afraid to express a different opinion

OR
- she contradicts her mother

      (20 points)
      = 20 marks

8.   Translate into English:

"Je suis descendue et . . . courait pas après . . ." (lines 10–12)   **10**
      (30)

Translation

I came downstairs

and I ran out of the house.

I even ran into the street,

as if I was running away from her . . .
        escaping

But of course she didn't run after me . . .

Passage 3

Le dimanche des enfants

1. Read the first paragraph. What two kinds of Sunday might Elodie have? Give details.   **2 points**
    - boring because her family relaxes
    - exciting because she devotes the day to her great love: drama

2. Olivia's weekends are different (lines 7–13).

    (a) Where does she go?   **2 points**
    - forest
    - a large, old house
    - in a mountain village
      (any 2)

    (b) Why does it feel like going on holiday?   **1 point**
    - her parents are not on at her to do her homework

    (c) Mention three activities she does there at different times of the year.   **3 points**
    - long games of Monopoly with her father in the Spring
    - looking under leaves for chestnuts in the Autumn
    - skiing in Winter

3. Ludovic comes from Vénissieux, a deprived part of Lyon (lines 14–19).

    (a) How does he occupy himself on his own?   **1 point**
    - he kicks the ball around (outside his flat)

    (b) What does he do if enough of his friends are available?   **1 point**
    - he has a game of football

    (c) What does he tell us about helping his parents on their allotment?   **3 points**
    - he watches them working more than he helps
    - he likes watering
    - he does not like pulling up the carrots

4. Mathieu spends a lot of time in front of the television (lines 23–30).
    What does he not like about Sylvester Stallone?   **2 points**
    - he thinks he is not a good actor
    - he does not like the way he speaks
    - he thinks the actor takes himself too seriously
      (any 2)

5.   Read paragraph 5.

   (a)   In what way has the divorce of Marie's parents had a positive effect on her Sundays?   **1 point**
   - she does twice as many things as she did before

   (b)   What does she do with her father?   **2 points**
   - she goes with him to his flying club
   - or they go walking together in the Alps

6.   From the final paragraph mention two things this particular parent does not enjoy at *Euro Disney*.   **2 points**
   - the queue at the ticket desks
   - the crush to see the big parade

   (20 points)

   = 20 marks

7.   Translate into English:

   "Et puis ... inviter mes copains."   (lines 20–22)   **10**

   (30)

   Translation

   Then there are the children who get bored because their parents are working, (work)

   like   Obé whose father is a taxi driver.
   such as

   "My parents want to sleep

   and I am not allowed

   to make any noise or invite my friends over."
                                               round

Passage 4

Mon père ne veut pas me laisser vivre ma vie

1. Olivia gets very good marks at school.

    (a) What is the one thing that Olivia's father has demanded of her since 1st year?   **1 point**
    - that she remains top of the class

    (b) What would her father like her to become?   **2 points**
    - a doctor
    - or a lawyer

2. Bernard Morel wants his daughter to be the best.
    What two things does Olivia have to do to please her father?   **2 points**
    - attend evening classes
    - do homework during the holidays

3. The tension between Olivia and her father increases when she finds her true vocation (lines 12–21).

    (a) When she started doing drama at school how did her father react?   **2 points**
    - he did not take her seriously at first
    - he thought it was just a passing phase
    - her increasing love of acting began to worry him
      (any 2)

    (b) How does he behave now after her drama class at school?   **1 point**
    - he sulks / he is childish

4. Bernard Morel is very particular about Olivia's friends.

    (a) In what way is Olivia critical of him in this respect.   **2 points**
    - she says that he judges her friends in 5 minutes
    - without taking the time to get to know them

    (b) How does he expect her friends to dress?   **2 points**
    - to wear a clean pair of jeans to the house
            an ironed shirt

5. Read paragraph 7.

    (a) Why did Olivia rebel against her father last summer?   **2 points**
         • he had enrolled her on a month's course in England
         • against her wishes

    (b) What were her own plans   **2 points**
         • to spend the holidays at the house of a friend's uncle
         • in the south of France

    (c) On holiday in what way did she punish her father?   **1 point**
         • she never got in touch

6. In the final paragraph Olivia reveals her plans for the future.

    (a) What is going to be the most difficult thing for her?   **2 points**
         • to get her father to accept the idea that she wants to study drama
         • to tell him that she has already passed the entrance exam

    (b) What is she prepared to do to finance her studies?   **1 point**
         • work in a fast-food restaurant

                                                                              (20 points)

                                                                              = 20 marks

7. Translate into English:

    "La semaine dernière . . . c'est regrettable!"   (lines 27–30).   **10**

                                                                                        (30)

Translation

"Last week she told my father that

I was (in the middle of) working away at my maths
                                        slaving

                  whereas
with a friend while (in actual fact)

I had gone to see a play.

We always have to lie to him and this is regrettable!"
                                        unfortunate

60

Passage 5

On boit trop dans les fêtes

1. In the first paragraph we are given information about young people and alcohol.

    (a) What did 42% of adolescents reveal in a recent survey?   **3 points**
        - they claimed to have had at least one alcoholic drink
        - in the last week
        - the vast majority of them had drunk at a party

    (b) What are we told about one in three of those surveyed?   **1 point**
        - they claimed to have been drunk

2. According to the school nurse, why do some pupils leave the class?   **2 points**
        - they have a sore head
        - they feel sick

3. The author suggests why young people drink at parties (lines 10–15).

    (a) How can alcohol help certain individuals?   **2 points**
        - a drink puts them into the party mood
        - it helps them to socialise / prevents them being on their own in a
          corner

    (b) According to the author, why do some people drink lots on a regular basis? **3 points**
        - to have the courage to ask girls to dance
        - to have the nerve to talk to others / to join in the conversation
        - to be like their friends
        - to feel part of a group
          (any 3)

4. Cécile tells us about a bad experience she had at a party (lines 16–24).

    (a) Why did she drink alcohol?   **1 point**
        - everyone else was drinking (to be like everyone else)

    (b) What two other things did she do which she regrets?   **2 points**
        - she smoked
        - she started babbling (talking about anything)

    (c) Where did she spend the rest of the evening?   **2 points**
        - stretched out
        - on the balcony

5. The author suggests you follow Géraldine's example.
    What does she do?   **2 points**
    - she only has one alcoholic drink
    - the rest of the evening she drinks sparkling mineral water

6. The author gives the reader advice (lines 32–39).

    (a)   When should you leave a party?   **1 point**
    - when your friends start to raid father's drinks cabinet / bar

    (b)   What should you agree on with your friends prior to the party? **1 point**
    - at least one person in the group should stay sober

                                                                (20 points)

                                                                = 20 marks

7. Translate into English:

    "Mon père est venu . . . mal de tête infernal." (lines 21–23).   **10**

                                                                             (30)

Translation

My father came to collect me in an unbelievable state!

The worst thing is that I told him

everything I had said and done.

The next day I scarcely dared look him straight in the face.
                                                        eye

I had a splitting headache.
         dreadful

Passage 6

C'est la rentrée!

1. Read the first paragraph. Give two reasons why some 6 year old pupils are unhappy at school. **2 points**
    - it separates them from their parents
    - they are afraid of it

2. A pupil lacking motivation is different.
    Why does he go to school? **3 points**
    - he goes out of habit
    - to see his friends
    - he has to go somewhere

3. Truancy is on the increase.
    What statistics are we given in the third paragraph concerning occasional and frequent absenteeism? **2 points**
    - one in two pupils is absent occasionally
    - one in ten is absent on a regular basis

4. Odile has difficulty motivating her pupils (lines 13–22).

    (a) Why does she find it so hard? **3 points**
    - many of her pupils' parents are unemployed
    - they hear of those who have their baccalauréat
    - just managing to get work as supermarket checkout assistants

    (b) What is the most important thing Odile wants to teach her pupils at the start of the school year? **2 points**
    - to get up in silence when she comes into the room
    - not to forget their books and jotters

5. Read paragraph 6.

    (a) What does Anne say to encourage her pupils? **3 points**
    - if they have a problem
    - they should ask for help
    - if she has to explain something three times she will do it

    (b) How do pupils like to be treated? **1 point**
    - like adults (not like kids)

6.   Carole appears quite realistic (lines 29–35).

        What does she tell herself about adolescents?   **2 points**

- you cannot expect them to be interested in everything
- all the time

7.   In the final paragraph we are given Lucile's impression of her teacher.

        (a)   Why did she think her teacher was on the verge of a breakdown last year?   **1 point**

- she trembled the whole year in front of the class

        (b)   What evidence is there that the pupils did not learn much?   **1 point**

- during her lessons they played cards more often than they took notes

                                                       (20 points)

                                                       = 20 marks

8.   Translate into English:

        "Travaillons! . . . le roman de *Don Quichotte*." (lines 30–33)   **10**

                                                          (30)

Translation

Let's work!

She also shows a certain detachment;

"I take my subject seriously,

but I don't get angry if two pupils laugh stupidly

while I am talking to them about love in the novel *Don Quichotte*."

Passage 7

Directrice d'hôtel

1. In paragraph 1 we are told how Annie spends the first part of her day.

    (a) What is the very first thing she does? **2 points**
    - she goes to greet (say hello to) her guests having breakfast
    - to check that all is well

    (b) What does she discuss with her regulars? **1 point**
    - their plans for the day

    (c) Why does she then go to reception? **1 point**
    - to receive guests who want to pay their bill

2. The bedrooms have to be seen to (lines 7–10).

    (a) What does she go over with the chambermaids? **3 points**
    - the reservations
    - the number of vacant rooms
    - those which have to be cleaned first

    (b) Mention three things which could spoil the hotel's image. **3 points**
    - a burst lightbulb
    - a leak
    - a faulty TV

3. Read paragraph 3.

    (a) What does Annie discuss with the chef? **2 points**
    - what the service has been like the day before
    - the quality of the dishes / courses
    - the clients' comments
      (any 2)

    (b) Apart from fellow hoteliers, who does Annie meet up with when she goes to the market? **1 point**
    - her suppliers

4. Annie also has administrative work to do (lines 22–26).

    (a) What exactly keeps her busy in her office? **2 points**
    - the accounts
    - filing documents

    (b) What determines how much money she makes daily? **1 point**
    - she makes more if she organises a banquet

5. Annie sorts out her business with her accountant (lines 27–32).

    (a) What does she need to renegotiate?   **1 point**
    - the interest rate on a bank loan

    (b) Why is it important for her to invest in the business?   **2 points**
    - to improve its service
    - to remain in the 2-star category

6. Annie continues to work into the evening (lines 33–41).
    What is the last thing she does before leaving?   **1 point**
    - she checks the list of guests' check-outs and reservations

                                                                                (20 points)

                                                                                = 20 marks

7. Translate into English:

    "une dizaine . . . le tour des tables." (lines 18–20)   **10**

                                                                                (30)

Translation

About ten tables are occupied.

The place enjoys a good reputation.

Apart from the chef, an assistant and a dishwasher are busy in the kitchen,
                                                              bustle   about
                                                              bustling about

while three people are serving in the dining room.
                        serve

Annie goes round the tables.

Passage 8

Je travaille sur quatre jours

1. Martine decided to work part-time.

   (a) What prompted this decision? **2 points**
   - she had a baby (girl)
   - she wanted time for herself to see to the baby

   (b) How did her husband respond to her working part-time? **2 points**
   - his reaction was: "Why not?" (he did not mind)
   - there was no argument (they did not fight over the decision)

2. Véronique tells us what life used to be like before she worked a 4-day week.

   (a) How was her working week? **3 points**
   - she never had any time
   - everything went by too fast
   - she did not socialise during the week (see anyone)
   - she did not do anything during the week
     (any 3)

   (b) What can she do now on a Friday? **2 points**
   - go shopping
   - go to the hairdresser's

   (c) Mention two things she can now do at the weekend. **2 points**
   - train to climb
   - go jogging
   - go to the swimming-pool
   - go to the mountains for three days
     (any 2)

   (d) Her salary has been cut. Why does she not see this as a problem? **1 point**
   - She has no-one to support (no dependents)

3. Hugues mentions his circumstances.

   (a) Why does he work a 4-day week? **1 point**
   - it was a company decision, not his choice

   (b) What does he do with his extra time? **2 points**
   - he works on the house (does DIY)
   - he works on the children's games room
   - he works on the fences (any 2)

   (c) Hugues' family lifestyle has not changed. He mentions one difference. What is it? **1 point**
   - they save less

4.   Bernard lives in the country.

  (a)   So that his children can take part in different activities, what does he have to do?   **1 point**
  • spend lots of time driving them around

  (b)   As none of his children has school on Saturday morning, what will this allow the
      family to do?   **1 point**
  • go away for the weekend on Friday evening

  (c)   Mention two things Bernard does at his club.   **2 points**
  • he plays all kinds of music on the piano every week
  • twice a month they give concerts

                                                                                  (20 points)

                                                                                  = 20 marks

5.   Translate into English:

        "Je ne pêche pas . . . pommes de terre." (lines 22–25)   **10**

                                                                                  (30)

Translation

I don't fish, I don't hunt either. I don't read a lot.

On Sunday we go for a walk.
                    walks

We go to the seaside but I cannot swim.

Next Spring I shall do the garden round the house.

I shall put in tomatoes and potatoes.
      plant

Passage 9

Les ambitions des jeunes

1. Nathalie has to work harder than others in training for the French horse-riding championships.
   Why is this?   **2 points**
   - the others will see the difficulties
   - Nathalie is practically blind (she can only make out shadows)

2. Nathalie was unlike most other little girls. How do you know this?   **2 points**
   - when she was young she did not play with dolls
   - but with model horses or farms

3. Two things might have put her off training professionally (lines 9–12).
   Mention two obstacles.   **3 points**
   - her parents' lack of money (both working class)
   - the rebuff of one of her first trainers
   - who thought she would never make it

4. Nathalie trains intensively.
   How does she manage the jumps?   **1 point**
   - she guesses them

5. Read paragraph 5. Nathalie leaves a special school to study in mainstream education.

   (a) What help is she given in school?   **2 points**
   - a braille writing machine
   - cassettes

   (b) What evidence is there that she is successful at this school?   **1 point**
   - she goes on to university
   OR
   - she goes on to study Italian and Spanish

6. Sophie is determined to work in the aeronautics industry in Britain (lines 23–33).

   (a) Why does the author consider this to be practically impossible?   **3 points**
   - she is a woman and French
   - she wants to work in an organisation which employs 99% men
   - all of whom are English

   (b) Her ambition does not stop there. What are her future plans?   **1 point**
   - to work in Canada or Australia

7.   Toussaint is a successful producer of computer software (lines 34–42).

    (a)   What would surprise a lot of people about him?   **1 point**
- he is only 17

    (b)   What does his software allow you to do?   **2 points**
- draw family trees
- produce statistics on your ancestors

    (c)   What are his future plans?   **1 point**
- to bring out an improved version of his computer software

    (d)   Why is he having to repeat a school year?   **1 point**
- he did not have time to study

                                                             (20 points)

                                                            = 20 marks

8.   Translate into English:

      "il y a seulement . . . fait que commencer." (lines 28–31)   **10**
                                                                      (30)

Translation

There are only four women, and one French woman: Sophie.

Her British colleagues, a bit cold   at first,
                              standoffish

quickly adopt her,
       adopted

even as a Sunday golfing partner (on Sundays).

But she is only just beginning.

70

Passage 10

Prof de banlieue

1. The teacher does not like Mondays. Why not?   **2 points**
   - a whole week lies ahead
   - of screaming pupils
   - of written work to be marked
   - of headaches
     (any 2)

2. When her pupils come into the classroom they appear quite unruly (lines 7–11).
   Mention three things they do before sitting down.   **3 points**
   - they scribble on the board
   - they fiddle with the tape recorder
   - they stroke the teacher's hair
   - they ask her if she has just washed her hair   (any 3)

3. Read paragraph 3.

   (a) In what way does Mohand interrupt the lesson?   **1 point**
   - he squeals (like a pig)

   (b) Why is the teacher particularly annoyed with this interruption?   **2 points**
   - she was concentrating on explaining a grammar point
   - she had the attention of the whole class

   (c) What action does she take when he swears at her?   **1 point**
   - she reports him

4. The headmaster comes into the classroom (lines 18–29).

   (a) How does he punish Mohand?   **2 points**
   - Mohand is summoned before the teacher (in front of the class)
   - he is made to apologize appropriately to the teacher

   (b) The headmaster reminds the class of the basic school rules. What are they?   **2 points**
   - to respect teachers and friends
   - to work hard

   (c) What sort of background do these pupils come from?   **3 points**
   - immigrant families
   - unemployed
   - poor (on a low income)

   (d) What touching gesture does Mohand make towards his teacher at the end of the lesson?   **2 points**
   - he gives her a note
   - in which he writes that he likes her

5. The lesson is interrupted again (lines 30–35).
   Why do the pupils have to leave the classroom at 11.33? **1 point**
   - there is a fire in the corridor

6. In the final paragraph we are told of the pupils' dreams. What do they hope for? **1 point**
   - a nicc job

   (20 points)

   = 20 marks

7. Translate into English:

   "Les élèves prennent . . . et enthousiastes." (lines 36–38) **10**
   (30)

Translation

The pupils take the test seriously for (because) it is difficult.

Sitting (seated) at my desk I watch them work.

They are no longer laughing.

I (do) like them.

They are hard-working and enthusiastic.

Passage 11

Vivre à Londres

1. Christophe is now working in London.

   (a) How did he find out about his current job?   **2 points**
   - he saw an advertisement
   - in an employment agency / job centre (in Marseille)

   (b) Why was he attracted to the post?   **3 points**
   - he wanted a new experience
   - he wanted to learn English
   - he wanted to drive a double-decker

   (c) What is the only problem in his new job?   **2 points**
   - he does not understand the passengers' questions
   - as they do not all speak Oxford English

2. In the second paragraph Hélène Verdier, another expatriate living in London, suggests why there used to be so few French people working for British cinema and television. What reason does she give?   **1 point**
   - they had insufficient command of the English language (they did not master the language)

3. Read paragraph 3. What are we told about the 180 000+ young French people who come to work in London?   **3 points**
   - they come mostly for quite a short period
   - from 3 months to 2 years
   - 80% come to work in restaurants and hotels

4. François is an actor from Paris.

   (a) How do you know that he had a successful lifestyle and career?   **2 points**
   - he had a comfortable salary
   - he had a nice flat
   - he was offered lots of parts
     (any 2)

   (b) How does he earn extra cash in London?   **2 points**
   - childminds / babysits for
   - several well-off families

5.   Read lines 30 to 34. According to Olivier, why is an employee who works late not highly regarded in Britain?   **1 point**
            • he will be seen as the one who did not know how to organise his day

6.   In paragraph 6 we are told of the disadvantages of living in London.

    (a)   What might determine where a French family lives?   **1 point**
      • the proximity of the French school (in Kensington)

    (b)   Why might living in Kensington be out of the question?   **1 point**
      • the rents are exorbitant (grossly excessive)
      (it is a well-to-do area)

7.   Gilles preferred to buy his London home rather than rent.
    What other considerable family expense does he mention?   **1 point**
      • school fees

8.   What conclusion does the author draw in her final comment?   **1 point**
      • you can live in London, but at a price
          it is costly

                                      (20 points)

                                      = 20 marks

9.   Translate into English:

      "Ici à Londres . . . cinéma!" (lines 10–13)   **10**
                                          (30)

Translation

Here in London the French are everywhere.

They work in restaurants and night clubs,

as well as in banks and insurance companies,

not forgetting football teams

and even the film industry!

Passage 12

Je gagne plus en un mois que mon père en un an

1. Lee Sung-Hee no longer recognises Seoul.
    What change has she seen in the last 40 years?   **2 points**
    - at the start of the 60s South Korea was an agricultural country
    - now it is the 11th most industrialised power in the world

2. She mentions what life used to be like (lines 5–10).

    (a) How does she describe her house?   **2 points**
    - it had one room
    - it had a thatched roof

    (b) Why was it fortunate that her family were fishermen?   **1 point**
    - there was always fish to eat

    (c) Why was she never unhappy?   **1 point**
    - this was the only life she knew

3. We are told about her son, Park Chon-Soo (lines 11–20).

    (a) What was South Korea like just after he was born?   **2 points**
    - the country was ruined
    - famine raged
    - the country only survived thanks to international aid
    (any 2)

    (b) Why did the country embark on a massive education programme?   **1 point**
    - 75% of the population was illiterate

    (c) Why was Park Chon-Soo forbidden access to higher education?   **2 points**
    - due to his social background
    - sons of unskilled workers or peasants were not allowed to go to university

4. We are told about Confucius' influence (lines 21–24).

    (a) Who exactly was he?   **2 points**
    - a Chinese thinker
    - of the 6th century B.C.

    (b) What is his school of thought?   **3 points**
    - to respect work
    - to want education
    - family solidarity
    - loyalty towards one's country
    (any 3)

5.   For many people working conditions improved in 70s Korea (lines 25–31).

   (a)   In what way was Park Chon-Soo better off than his father had been?   **1 point**
       • he earned more in one month than his father in one year
   OR
       • salaries rose quickly

   (b)   When did he first become aware of his prosperity?   **1 point**
       • when he was able to buy toilet paper

6.   In the final paragraph we are told what things are like today for the Park family.

   (a)   What is Park Soo-Kyong now interested in?   **1 point**
       • fashion and singers

   (b)   In what way has he had more opportunities than his father?   **1 point**
         • he has been accepted into the maths faculty
           (he has been able to go to university)

                                                            (20 points)

                                                            = 20 marks

7.   Translate into English:

   "A cette époche . . . habitaient en ville." (lines 6–8)   **10**

                                                            (30)

Translation

At that time Korea was occupied by Japan.
   the

I only had two outfits when I was little.

We did not have any money,

but I was never hungry,

unlike those who lived in the town.

Passage 13

La nouvelle Chine

1. Kim is one of the new Chinese generation.
    Where has she been working for the last six months?   **1 point**
    - a small computing company in Peking

2. In the second paragraph we are told something about recent Chinese history.

    (a) What exactly is the "loi de l'enfant unique"?   **3 points**
    - a law
    - which prohibits Chinese couples
    - from having more than one child

    (b) What does Kim do in the evening?   **1 point**
    - she attends computing classes

    (c) What does she hope to do one day?   **1 point**
    - start up her own company

3. There are drawbacks to the booming Chinese economy.
    What is the problem in Peking city centre today?   **1 point**
    - traffic jams

4. Twenty years ago nothing much would happen in Chinese cities after 6.30pm. How have
    things changed?   **2 points**
    - shopping centres open late
    - there are trendy restaurants and discos

5. Wu Lan realises that her generation is lucky compared to her parents' (lines 21–25).

    (a) Why does she feel so fortunate?   **3 points**
    - her parents worked their whole life
    - for a low wage (miserable salary)(a pittance)
    - they had no free time
    - they had no freedom
      (any 3)

    (b) What did her mother work as?   **1 point**
    - primary school teacher

6.   Wu Lan has a boyfriend. In China showing affection in public is no longer taboo. How are
     Wu Lan and her boyfriend able to show their feelings for each other?   **2 points**
              • they can hold hands in the street
              • kiss in the park

7.   We are told about young people in Shanghai (lines 34 46).

     (a)   Where does Chang Yie go to have fun?   **2 points**
              • bowling
              • cybercafé

     (b)   Mention two things Chang Yie and his girlfriend might do on the net.   **2 points**
              • look for a job
              • go through the advertisements to buy a car / flat
              • send messages to friends abroad
              • have a "conversation" about all kinds of things
                (any 2)

     (c)   Why are the Australian and American university websites appreciated by Chinese
             internet surfers?   **1 point**
              • they can consult the entrance requirements

                                                                                            (20 points)

                                                                                            = 20 marks

8.   Translate into English:

         "Les Chinois aiment . . . de cuir." (lines 17–20)   **10**

                                                                                                (30)

   ## Translation

         (The) Chinese like buying.   In their brand new apartments
                          shopping   split   flats

         all the new owners have   a television,
         the new owners all possess

         (another   one for the only child),
          an additional

         a video recorder (or more often a DVD player),

         a fridge-freezer, a washing machine and a leather sofa.

Passage 14

Le tour du monde à vélo

1. Claude and Françoise have the crazy idea of going round the world on a bike.

   (a) Why do they dismiss the idea of travelling by motorbike or on foot?   **2 points**
   - by motorbike is too expensive
   - on foot is too slow

   (b) What slight problem do they foresee?   **1 point**
   - they have never cycled

   (c) Mention three things they have to do in preparation for their journey.   **3 points**
   - find good bikes
   - save up
   - prepare the itinerary (decide on the route)
   - find out about the different destinations
   - be vaccinated
   - learn English
   (any 3)

2. Claude and Françoise go to Nepal.

   (a) With whom do they spend Christmas Eve?   **2 points**
   - a couple and
   - about 50 orphans

   (b) What surprise is in store for them?   **2 points**
   - Father Christmas arrives
   - on an elephant

3. Their adventure continues in Thailand.

   (a) What happens to them in the south of the country?   **2 points**
   - they are held up at gunpoint
   - by two youths on motorbikes

   (b) How is the situation resolved?   **2 points**
   - a few minutes later lorries arrive
   - the bandits flee on their motorbikes

4. In Australia Françoise gets pregnant. How does this affect their journey?   **3 points**
    - it does not change anything
    - a trailer is attached to Françoise's bike
    - they have to carry a few more bags

5. In the final paragraph we are told why Claude and Françoise feel the trip was worth it. Give three reasons.   **3 points**
    - they have learned to be tolerant
    - to accept people without judging them
    - to take the time to observe the world

(20 points)

= 20 marks

6. Translate into English:

    "Lorsque des amis . . . Ils ont tort." (lines 36–38)   **10**

    (30)

Translation

When friends or curious people ask Claude and Françoise
                    interested

what frightened them most,
      scared

they expect answers like

disease, dangerous animals and theft.
diseases   robbery

They are wrong.

Passage 15

Manger à sa faim

1. Pema is very hungry.
    What is the staple diet in his family?   **2 points**
    - a mixture of potatoes
    - and rice

2. Pema and his family have had to leave their homeland (lines 5–10).

    (a) Why is this?   **3 points**
    - China occupies Tibet
    - the Tibetans are forbidden to live according to their traditions
    - for this reason many Tibetans live elsewhere

    (b) We are told that the soil in Pema's new homeland is not fertile. What other reason is
    given for the immediate shortage of food?   **1 point**
    - the last corn (maize) harvest was destroyed by a cyclone

3. What are we told about meat in paragraph 3?   **2 points**
    - much too expensive
    - they can only have it once or twice a month

4. Many of Pema's friends are ill (lines 15–17).
    What alarming fact is revealed about Tenzin?   **1 point**
    - he is 12 but looks 8

5. Read paragraph 5. We are told about the importance of good food.

    (a) Why is it essential?   **2 points**
    - for growth
    - to be healthy

    (b) According to the text what exactly is malnutrition?   **2 points**
    - not having <u>enough</u> to eat
    - not having a <u>varied</u> enough diet

    (c) Mention the two diseases caused by lack of vitamin A and iodine.   **2 points**
    - eye diseases (due to lack of vitamin A)
    - mental retardation (due to lack of iodine)

    (d) What statistic are we presented with at the end of this paragraph?   **1 point**
    - in the world today one child in three is not fed enough

6.   Our planet produces enough food for all of its inhabitants.
     Why are there still starving children in the world, especially in Africa and Asia?   **2 points**
        • they live in poor countries or with poor families
        • their parents do not have money to buy food

7.   Pema reveals his dream in the final paragraph.
     What is it?   **2 points**
        • that his father will be able to work and earn enough money one day
        • to feed the whole family himself

                                                                          (20 points)

                                                                          = 20 marks

8.   Translate into English:

        "Beaucoup d'enfants . . . leurs enfants." (lines 30–33)   **10**

                                                                          (30)

Translation

Lots of children are also victims of war(s) or political conflicts.

Their families, like Pema's, leave their villages and take refuge elsewhere.

The parents lose their job or the land

they used to cultivate
     cultivated

and become too poor to feed their children properly.

DIRECTED WRITING

ADVICE TO CANDIDATES

✧ Read through the whole scenario carefully. It is imperative that you include all the information correctly and that you make reference to each bullet point. Some bullet points may require you to give more than one piece of information.

✧ Tick off each bullet point once you have written down the appropriate information. You may find that in the first two bullet points you are able to include all the relevant information in just a couple of lines.

✧ Always refer back to the scenario in the introduction. It is important that you give the correct information, e.g., if it is specified that you went to France last summer for two weeks, you must convey this information exactly, or if it states that you travelled by bus and ferry, you must not write that you went by train through the Eurotunnel.

✧ Remember too that you are encouraged to give any other relevant details. This is your opportunity to show off the French you know and to incorporate any relevant expressions you have learned during the year.

✧ Restrict your use of a dictionary to looking up key words required to convey the message in any of the bullet points or in the scenario, e.g., a choir, a restaurant, a concert, to go camping, etc., and for checking the spellings and genders of what you have already written.

✧ Read through your piece of writing once you have finished and check agreements, e.g., *une grande maison*, verb forms, e.g., *je suis allé* and all genders, e.g.. *le / la gîte*. If you have time, read through the scenario again and make sure that you have included all the appropriate information.

✧ There is no advantage in exceeding the word limit. Provided you have included all the points accurately, credit will be given.

✧ Time yourself. Make sure you can complete the task in 40 minutes.

THE MARKING OF THE DIRECTED WRITING

You are awarded a pegged mark out of 15 for this paper. A very good piece of writing will be awarded 15 / 15, a good piece of writing will be awarded 12 / 15, a satisfactory effort will be awarded 9 / 15, an unsatisfactory attempt will be given 6 / 15, a poor piece of work will be awarded 3/15 and a very poor attempt will be given no marks. For every bullet point omitted, two raw marks will be deducted. (Therefore, if you produce a 'good' piece of writing — 12 / 15 — but omit one bullet point your final score will be 10 / 15. If you miss out three or more bullet points you will be awarded no marks.)

To score highly in this paper you need to demonstrate a high level of accuracy, communicate clearly throughout and include all the information that is required. My advice is to practise writing as many different scenarios as possible during the year, paying close attention to the mistakes that you are making so that they do not recur in a subsequent piece of writing. On the day of the examination include all the bullet points, but write only what you know to be correct.

DIRECTED WRITING 1

Last summer you worked in France for two months before going to university. Towards the end of your stay you met a young French person who was considering finding a summer job in Britain.

On your return, you write to him / her, **in French**, to tell him / her of your experiences.

You must include the following information and **you should try to add** other relevant details:

- where you stayed in France and for how long

- where you worked and what you thought of the job

- the hours you worked and how you got on with your boss

- how you spent your free time

- any aspects of your stay you did not enjoy

- whether you would recommend working abroad

Your account should be 150–180 words in length.   **(15)**

DIRECTED WRITING 2

Last Easter you spent a fortnight with your pen friend in France. You travelled there by train and by boat. You spent one week at his / her home. During this time you met all of his / her friends. The second week you went camping with your pen friend and his / her family.

Now you have been asked to write an account of your experiences **in French** for inclusion in the foreign language section of your school / college magazine.

You must include the following information and **you should try to add** other relevant details:

- how you travelled to France and what you did during the journey

- who was in his / her family and how you got on with them

- what your pen friend's home was like

- what you did with your pen friend the first week

- whether you enjoyed the camping trip

- whether you would go back to stay with them again

Your account should be 150–180 words in length. **(15)**

DIRECTED WRITING 3

Last June a group of French pupils / students came to your school / college on an exchange trip for 10 days. One of them stayed with you. The French students spent one day in your school / college.

You have been chosen to write a report of the trip, **in French**, to send to the exchange school / college.

You must include the following information and **you should try to add** other relevant details:

- who stayed with you and for how long

- what the French person thought of your home

- what he / she thought of your school / college

- what else you did together during his / her stay

- what he / she disliked about Scotland

- whether you plan to visit him / her in France

Your account should be 150–180 words in length. **(15)**

DIRECTED WRITING 4

Last summer a French choir came to stay and to perform in your town for three days. Your family offered to host two of the choir members. As you are the only French speaker in the family, you agreed to help out, to go with them to some concerts in the evening and to show them the sights in your town in the afternoon.

You have been asked by the choirmaster to write a report, **in French**, for his community magazine.

You must include the following information and **you should try to add** other relevant details:

- who exactly came to stay and for how long

- what they thought of Scottish food

- what you did with them in the afternoons

- what you thought of their concerts

- if you enjoyed their stay

- whether you would play host again

Your account should be 150–180 words in length. (15)

DIRECTED WRITING 5

Last October you went on a school trip to Paris for five days. You travelled by bus and overnight ferry with six teachers and 47 of your classmates. You stayed in a youth hostel in the centre of the city. One day you went on an excursion to the town of Chartres to visit the cathedral.

On your return you are asked to write a report of your trip, **in French**, for inclusion in the school magazine.

You must include the following information and **you should try to add** other relevant details:

- who went on the trip and how long you were away

- how you travelled and what you did during the journey

- where you stayed and what you thought of the accommodation

- what you did during your stay

- how you got on with your friends and teachers

- whether you would go on a school trip in the future

Your account should be 150–180 words in length.   **(15)**

DIRECTED WRITING 6

Last year you went to Canada to study in a French-speaking school / college. You shared a flat in Montréal with three other students. You attended school every day and at the weekends and holidays you went travelling with your flatmates.

On your return you are asked to write a report, **in French**, of your year abroad for the Canadian school magazine.

You must include the following information and **you should try to add** other relevant details:

- where you stayed and with whom you shared

- which subjects you studied

- how this school compares with your own school / college

- how you organised the cooking and the housework in your flat

- what you did at weekends and during the holidays

- if you would recommend a year abroad to prospective students

Your account should be 150–180 words in length. (15)

DIRECTED WRITING 7

Last summer you went on a family holiday. Your family rented a gîte in the south of France and you spent three weeks there. During your stay you met others of the same age and spent some time with them. During the day you went to the beach with your family or went shopping, and in the evening you went out with your friends.

Now you have been asked to write about your experiences, **in French**, for your French class.

You must include the following information and **you should try to add** other relevant details:

- with whom you went and how long you stayed

- where you stayed and what you thought of the accommodation

- what you did to help your family with the housework

- what you did during the day

- what you did with your friends in the evening

- whether you would like to go on holiday with your family again

Your account should be 150–180 words in length. (15)

DIRECTED WRITING 8

Last winter you went on a school skiing trip to Val d'Isère in the French Alps for a week. You flew to Lyon and then took a coach to your 3-star hotel. You travelled with 19 other pupils and 4 teachers. You went skiing during the day, although the weather was bad. In the evening you went out with your friends in the village.

On your return, you are asked to write about the trip, **in French**, for your school magazine.

You must include the following information and **you should try to add** other relevant details:

- where exactly you went and who went with you

- where you stayed and with whom you shared a room

- what the weather was like

- what you did during your stay

- how you spent the evenings

- if you would recommend a school skiing trip to other pupils

Your account should be 150–180 words in length.   **(15)**

DIRECTED WRITING 9

Last Easter you travelled alone to France to visit a Scottish friend who was studying at Rennes university. You flew to Paris and then took the train to the city of Rennes. Your friend was ill while you were there and you had to go sightseeing on your own. On your return journey your flight was delayed for four hours.

Now you are writing to a French friend, **in French**, to tell him / her about your trip.

You must include the following information and **you should try to add** other relevant details:

- why you went to France and how you travelled

- what sightseeing you did during your stay in Rennes

- what you did to help your friend

- if you enjoyed spending so much time on your own

- what you did at the airport on your return journey

- what you learned from the whole experience

Your account should be 150–180 words in length.   **(15)**

DIRECTED WRITING 10

Last Christmas you and a friend organised a party for a group of Belgian pupils / students who had been on an exchange trip to your school. It was the last night of the Belgians' stay in Scotland.

You are asked to write a report about the evening, **in French**, for the school magazine.

You must include the following information and **you should try to add** other relevant details:

- where the party took place and how many people you invited

- what you and your friend did to organise it

- what you wore to the party

- how the evening went

- if you and your friend enjoyed the party

- what you did to tidy up after the party was over

Your account should be 150–180 words in length. (15)

DIRECTED WRITING PHRASES

Each of the following phrases relates directly to the bullet points in the Directed Writing tasks in this book. If you are having difficulty in expressing the message required in one of the bullet points, you will find an example of an appropriate phrase under the following headings:

- ✧ expressing when you went
- ✧ expressing where you went and with whom / who came to stay
- ✧ expressing how you travelled
- ✧ expressing what you did during the journey
- ✧ expressing how long you stayed
- ✧ expressing where you stayed
- ✧ describing your accommodation
- ✧ expressing how you got on with people
- ✧ giving your general opinion of your stay
- ✧ expressing what you did (on one occasion)
- ✧ expressing what you did (on more than one occasion)
- ✧ expressing likes and dislikes
- ✧ suggesting whether or not you would repeat the experience
- ✧ giving a reason for your opinion
- ✧ describing the job you did
- ✧ describing the weather

These phrases are not a substitute for learning the grammar rules, but they will provide emergency help for anyone who is working alone on these papers. Of course, once you use any of the phrases you need to learn it so that if you are required to write something similar in the future, you will know the expression.

In the initial stages of Directed Writing, you may need to refer to many of these phrases and integrate them into your own French. As the Higher year progresses, however, and you learn many of the expressions and become more confident in French, you should become less dependent on this section of the book.

DIRECTED WRITING PHRASES

The following phrases relate directly to the Directed Writing topics in this book and should help you to write your essay.

Expressing when you went

l'été dernier	last summer
l'hiver dernier	last winter
l'année dernière / l'an dernier	last year
pendant les vacances de Noël / Pâques	during the Christmas / Easter holidays
il y a deux ans	two years ago
en juin dernier	last June
à Noël dernier	last Christmas
à Pâques dernier	last Easter

Expressing where you went and with whom / who came to stay

je suis allé(e) en France	I went to France
on est allé(e)s au Canada	we went to Canada
nous sommes allé(e)s à Lyon	we went to Lyon
je suis resté(e) dans un petit village	I stayed in a small village
douze jeunes sont venu(e)s dans notre école en échange scolaire	12 young people came to our school on an exchange trip
je suis parti(e) en famille	I went away with my family
je suis parti(e) avec un groupe scolaire	I went away on a school trip
je suis parti(e) seul(e)	I went on my own
il y avait vingt personnes dans le groupe	there were 20 people in the group
nous avons loué un gîte dans le Midi	we rented a gîte in the south of France
on est allé(e)s faire du ski dans les Alpes	we went skiing in the Alps
une fille est restée chez moi	a girl stayed with me

Expressing how you travelled

on a voyagé par le train / en car	we travelled by train / by coach
on a pris le ferry de Douvres à Calais	we took the ferry from Dover to Calais
nous avons pris l'avion	we took the plane
nous avons voyagé par l'Eurotunnel	we went through the Eurotunnel
j'ai pris l'avion et le bateau	I took the plane and the boat

Expressing what you did during the journey

pendant le voyage je me suis endormi(e)	during the journey I fell asleep
j'ai parlé à d'autres voyageurs	I talked to other travellers
j'ai regardé par la fenêtre	I looked out of the window
j'ai passé mon temps à lire	I spent my time reading

Expressing how long you stayed

j'ai passé une semaine à Paris	I spent one week in Paris
on a passé quinze jours en France	we spent a fortnight in France
j'ai travaillé pendant deux mois en France	I worked for two months in France
je suis resté(e) quinze jours chez . . .	I stayed a fortnight with . . .
mon correspondant / ma correspondante	my pen friend

Expressing where you stayed

on a logé dans un hôtel trois étoiles	we stayed in a 3-star hotel
l'hôtel se trouvait dans une station de ski	the hotel was in a ski resort
on est restés dans une auberge de jeunesse	we stayed in a youth hostel
je suis resté(e) dans une famille française	I stayed with a French family
je suis allé(e) chez mon (ma) correspondant(e)	I went to my penfriend's house
il y avait quatre personnes dans la famille	there were four people in the family
on a fait du camping en pleine campagne	we went camping out in the country

Describing your accommodation

il / elle habitait une grande maison	he / she lived in a big house
l'hôtel était moche	the hotel was ugly
l'appartement était tout petit	the flat was tiny
j'ai partagé une chambre avec	I shared a room with

Expressing how you got on with people

je me suis très bien entendu(e) avec . . . la famille / mon patron / ses copains / copines	I got on really well with . . . the family / my boss / his / her friends
je ne me suis pas très bien entendu(e) avec . . .	I did not get on very well with . . .
je me suis fait des amis	I made friends
mon chef était très sympa	my boss was very nice

Giving your general opinion of your stay

je me suis beaucoup amusé(e)	I really enjoyed myself
on s'est bien amusés	we had great fun
je me suis un peu ennuyé(e)	I got a bit bored
j'avais le mal du pays	I felt homesick
ma famille m'a manqué	I missed my family
je me suis fait beaucoup d'ami(e)s	I made lots of friends
le travail était mal payé	the job was badly paid

Expressing what you did (on one occasion)

un jour j'ai fait les magasins	one day I went shopping
nous avons décidé d'organiser une fête	we decided to organise a party
un soir on est allé(e)s en boîte de nuit	we went clubbing one night
un matin je suis allé(e) en ville	one morning I went into town
je me suis perdu(e) en ville	I got lost in the town
le premier jour il / elle est venu(e) à mon école	the first day he / she came to my school

Expressing what you did (on more than one occasion)

j'allais souvent dans les cafés	I often went to cafés
je me couchais vers minuit d'habitude	I usually went to bed around midnight
il invitait souvent des amis à la maison	he often invited friends over
tous les soirs on mangeait à l'auberge de jeunesse	every evening we ate in the youth hostel
dans l'après-midi je me reposais	in the afternoon I relaxed
tous les matins je commençais mon travail à	every morning I started my work at
le matin je me bronzais sur la plage	in the morning I sunbathed on the beach
on sortait manger ensemble	we went out for a meal together
on faisait souvent du tourisme	we often went touring / sight-seeing
le week-end on visitait tous les monuments	at the weekend we visited all the sights
je nettoyais l'appartement	I cleaned the flat
chaque matin je passais l'aspirateur	every morning I did the vacuum cleaning
le soir j'aidais ma mère à préparer les repas	in the evening I helped my mother prepare the meals

Expressing likes and dislikes

je n'ai pas aimé la nourriture	I did not like the food
la nourriture était délicieuse	the food was delicious
on a très bien mangé	the food was very good
la famille était très gentille et accueillante	the family was very nice and welcoming
le travail était stressant	the work was stressful
il / elle a beaucoup aimé mon lycée	he / she really liked my school
il / elle n'a pas aimé la nourriture écossaise	he / she did not like Scottish food
ma maison lui plaisait beaucoup	he / she really liked my house

Suggesting whether or not you would repeat the experience

j'aimerais retourner à Paris	I'd like to go back to Paris
je n'aimerais pas retourner à Lyon	I would not like to go back to Lyon
je préférerais aller seul(e) ou avec des ami(e)s	I'd rather go on my own or with friends
je préférerais voyager en avion	I'd prefer to travel by plane
je recommanderais un séjour à l'étranger	I'd recommend a spell abroad
je n'y retournerais jamais	I'd never go back there
je ne repartirais jamais en famille	I'd never go away again with my family
je préférerais ne pas inviter un(e) Français(e) chez moi	I'd prefer not to invite a French person to my home

Giving a reason for your opinion

le voyage était trop long	the journey was too long
je ne me suis pas bien entendu avec la famille / les profs / mes camarades de classe	I did not get on well with the family / the teachers / my classmates
il faisait trop chaud pour moi	the weather was too hot for me
on n'avait rien en commun	we didn't have anything in common
les profs étaient trop sévères	the teachers were too strict
j'ai dépensé trop d'argent	I spent too much money
je me suis fait piquer par des moustiques	I was bitten by mosquitoes
j'ai eu un coup de soleil	I had sunburn
j'ai eu du mal à comprendre la langue	I had difficulty understanding the language
les Français parlent trop vite	the French talk too fast
du point de vue linguistique	from a linguistic point of view
j'ai beaucoup profité de mon séjour	I really made the most of my stay
la fête était un fiasco	the party was a disaster

Describing the job you did

j'ai travaillé comme plongeur/plongeuse	I worked as a dishwasher
serveur / serveuse	waiter / waitress
le travail était facile / difficile	the work was easy / hard
j'ai dû travailler dur	I had to work hard

Describing the weather

il faisait un temps splendide	the weather was marvellous
il neigeait tous les matins	it snowed every morning
il faisait beau la plupart du temps	the weather was nice most of the time
le soir il y avait de l'orage	it was stormy in the evening

END OF UNIT READING TESTS

LIFESTYLES

Passage 1

Appel à la tolérance

Non, Pierre Labrousse ne boit pas, ne se drogue pas et n'est pas contagieux. Si vous le voyez dans la rue, le visage blême ou le regard[1] vague, c'est qu'il vient de faire une crise d'épilepsie.

Épileptique depuis 14 ans, Pierre Labrousse a longtemps vécu sa maladie dans la peur. Les
5   premiers symptômes se révélaient par des malaises et des évanouissements. 4 ans plus tard Pierre souffre de crises violentes suivies de forts maux de tête. "Parfois, je perdais la mémoire et je fuguais sans savoir où j'allais. Je rentrais avec 4 kg de pain et 3 paquets de jambon!" Rapidement ses amis lui tournent le dos. "Ils pensaient que cette maladie était contagieuse ou que j'avais dû renoncer à l'alcool et qu'ils en voyaient les effets!"

10   Alors durant des années, Pierre a honte de sa maladie et se cache pour éviter le regard des autres. "Je ne voulais pas me donner en spectacle", avoue-t-il. Pour Fabienne, sa femme, la situation devient intolérable comme pour leurs deux enfants qui veulent sortir, jouer ou faire du sport avec leurs parents. Un soir, après le travail, Fabienne dit à son mari: "Ou tu sors avec moi, ou tu restes enfermé, sans moi!" Tendrement, Pierre ajoute: "Elle avait
15   raison. Si j'ai appris à accepter ma maladie, c'est grâce à[2] ma femme."

Approuvé par Tony, un ami épileptique présent lors de notre rencontre, Pierre précise: "Pour quelqu'un qui n'en a jamais vu, une crise d'épilepsie est très impressionnante, les muscles du malade sont tendus, les yeux roulent dans les orbites et le malade bave de la mousse. On en sort épuisé, comme si on avait fait 2 jours de ski sans discontinuer!" Un
20   jour, deux gendarmes soupçonnent même Pierre de s'être piqué dans des toilettes publiques alors qu'en réalité il vient de faire une crise.

Sous médicaments, Pierre se force à mener une vie régulière et saine. Il s'occupe du jardin et prépare les repas. "Certains jours je ne peux rien faire; interrompu par une crise, j'ai même brûlé un repas", dit-il en souriant. "Quand on est concentré on fait moins de crises,
25   ajoute Tony. Il faut s'occuper, suivre un programme. Chaque matin à 7h, je me lave et me rase avant d'entreprendre quelque chose."

Pour Pierre, vivre l'épilepsie, c'est l'accepter mais aussi en parler avec son entourage[3] et ne pas hésiter à le dire à son employeur si cela comporte un risque au travail. "En cas de crise, sachez qu'il ne faut pas lever le malade, ne rien lui donner à boire, éloigner les objets à sa portée tout en le laissant respirer librement. Et bien entendu, appeler une ambulance, un pharmacien ou un médecin."

30

[1] le regard: look
[2] grâce à: thanks to
[3] un entourage: circle of friends and family

Questions

1. *(a)* If you were to see Pierre in the street, what wrong conclusion might you draw?   **2 points**

   (b) Why would he be in this state?   **1 point**

2. *(a)* What were the first symptoms 14 years ago?   **2 points**

   (b) Mention two other symptoms which developed later.   **2 points**

   (c) Why did his friends turn their backs on him?   **2 points**

3. *(a)* Why was the situation especially difficult for his children?   **2 points**

   (b) What ultimatum did Fabienne finally give her husband?   **1 point**

4. *(a)* What happens when someone has an epileptic fit?   **3 points**

   (b) How do they feel after the fit?   **2 points**

5. Why were two policemen suspicious of Pierre?   **1 point**

6. Pierre tries to lead a normal, healthy life. What two things does he do?   **2 points**

7. How does Tony's daily routine begin?   **1 point**

8. What advice is given if you are present when someone is having a fit?   **3 points**

    24 points

Passage 2

Dans la peau d'un SDF[1]

Aujourd'hui, en France, 200 000 personnes vivent sans domicile fixe. Parmi eux, une grande majorité d'hommes célibataires. Mais il y a aussi des femmes SDF et de plus en plus de jeunes de moins de 25 ans.

«L'été, à part la peur de me faire agresser, je peux me débrouiller pour dormir dans la rue
5   ou dans un coin de square[2], raconte Bertrand. C'est quand il commence à faire froid que ça devient dur. On ne peut pas imaginer ce que c'est de grelotter toute la nuit, dans le vent, en essayant de se réchauffer dans un manteau troué. Ça me rend malade et ça me fatigue encore plus. Trouver un coin chaud et tranquille c'est presque impossible. Je me fais jeter par les concierges quand je m'endors dans un hall d'immeuble. J'ai essayé, une fois, de
10 dormir dans un centre commercial et les vigiles[3] m'ont frappé. La solution, c'est d'aller dormir dans un centre d'hébergement. Mais je n'aime pas ça. En général, il y a trop de monde pour moi dans le même dortoir. Il y a des bagarres, et je me suis même fait voler mes chaussures une nuit!»

Plusieurs associations servent des repas aux SDF. Les *Restos du cœur* sont ouverts du 15
15 décembre au 15 mars. L'année dernière, 59 millions de repas ont été distribués. 30 *Camions du cœur* traversent les grandes villes tous les soirs pour distribuer des repas chauds aux SDF. La majorité des plats viennent des stocks de l'Union européenne.

«Jamais je n'aurais cru que c'était si dur de vivre dans la rue, raconte Julien. Quand j'étais gamin, j'avais tellement peur à la maison que j'avais parfois envie de partir. Je
20 pensais trouver un petit peu de liberté à me promener toute la journée à ne rien faire et oublier. Je ne savais pas à quel point je me trompais. La rue, c'est comme la prison, sauf qu'il n'y a pas de murs. Je m'enferme dans ma tête, avec mes mauvais souvenirs. J'ai la sensation de les oublier quand je picole[4]. J'ai toujours picolé. Je ne vois pas d'autre solution. Aussi loin que je me rappelle, mon père buvait. Il rentrait ivre presque tous les
25 soirs. Alors il me battait. Pour un rien. Ma mère n'osait rien dire parce qu'elle avait peur. Elle a fini par faire semblant de ne plus rien voir. Ça donnait des envies de fuite. J'ai perdu mon boulot car j'étais souvent ivre et agressif. C'est pour les mêmes raisons que ma femme m'a jeté de notre appartement. Et là je me suis retrouvé dehors pour de bon, avec le pinard[5]; le plus mauvais compagnon que j'aie jamais eu.»

30 Beaucoup de SDF passent leurs journées à mendier dans les rues. Jean-Marc en a marre. «Je suis là, assis sur un banc ou par terre, je tends la main, et les passants défilent comme si je n'existais pas. C'est très rare que quelqu'un me parle et encore plus qu'il sourie. La plupart de ceux qui me parlent c'est pour me dire: "Trouvez du travail au lieu de rester dans la rue!"»

[1] un SDF: a homeless person
[2] un square: public gardens
[3] un vigile: a night watchman
[4] picoler: to booze
[5] le pinard: cheap wine

Questions

1. Who make up the 200 000 homeless people?   **3 points**

2. *(a)* Why does Bertrand find the winters so hard?   **2 points**

    (b) Why is he unable to sleep in the entrance hall of a block of flats?   **1 point**

    (c) What happened once when he tried to sleep in a shopping centre?   **1 point**

    (d) Why does he not like sleeping at a refuge centre?   **3 points**

3. Several organisations serve hot meals. Where does most of the food come
    from?   **1 point**

4. *(a)* As a child why did Julien sometimes feel like leaving home?   **1 point**

    (b) He feels imprisoned on the street. What keeps him trapped?   **1 point**

5. Mention three things we are told about his father.   **3 points**

6. How did Julien's wife end their relationship?   **1 point**

7. What does he say about the cheap wine that he drinks?   **1 point**

8. *(a)* What do passers-by generally do when Jean-Marc begs?   **2 points**

    (b) What comment might they make?   **2 points**

                                                                                      22 points

Passage 3

Le danger de la drogue

Stéphane est mort le 16 juin d'une overdose médicamenteuse. Il avait 19 ans . . . La dernière fois que nous avons eu notre fils au téléphone, c'était trois jours avant son décès[1]. Il nous a simplement dit qu'il sortait de l'hôpital, que tout allait bien, qu'il était en route pour Toulouse, comme prévu. Il disait que nous ne devions pas nous inquiéter, qu'il était
5   sorti d'affaire, que c'était bien fini.

Depuis, nous nous battons. Plus que tout, nous aimions notre fils. Aujourd'hui, nous cherchons à comprendre ce qui s'est passé. Pour que d'autres jeunes ne connaissent pas à leur tour le triste destin de Stéphane. Et pour que des parents ne vivent pas ce drame. Nous n'avons pas honte de dire que notre fils était un toxicomane[2]. Bien au contraire, nous
10   voulons briser un tabou et montrer aussi que cela peut arriver à n'importe qui.

C'était un enfant sensible[3], gentil et solitaire. Quand il était au collège, il avait d'assez mauvais résultats et ses copains laissaient à désirer. Il faisait l'école buissonnière[4], manquait ses cours pour aller à la pêche. C'est pourquoi, croyant bien faire, nous avons décidé de l'éloigner de cet environnement et de le mettre en internat à une vingtaine de
15   kilomètres de chez nous. Il a très mal pris cet éloignement, il s'est probablement senti rejeté.

Après quelques mois Stéphane a été expulsé de l'internat. Motif: il avait sniffé de la colle. Il avait 16 ans. Nous étions bouleversés. Plus tard, nous avons su que c'est à cette époque qu'il avait été initié par un copain aux drogues médicamenteuses. Nous avons essayé de
20   discuter avec lui, cherché à comprendre. Mais il ne nous écoutait pas.

A 17 ans, il en a terminé avec la scolarité. Il a trouvé un boulot d'apprenti cuisinier et continué à fréquenter les mêmes copains. Il a adopté le look punk, et puis il y a eu ce chagrin d'amour avec sa petite amie. Alors, par moments, il trouvait refuge et réconfort dans l'alcool et les médicaments. Il avait des hallucinations, devenait agressif. En février, il
25   a cassé une vitrine avec un copain pour voler de la colle et plus d'un an plus tard, on l'a retrouvé dans le coma au milieu de la rue. Il a été hospitalisé.

Et puis nous avons reçu ce dernier coup de fil. Juste avant sa mort. Il voulait sans doute nous rassurer. Le 16 juin, nous avons même reçu une carte postale: "Tout va bien. Je suis en route pour Toulouse." Mais le même jour, un policier frappait à notre porte pour nous
30   annoncer la mort de notre fils.

[1] le décès: death
[2] un toxicomane: a drug addict
[3] sensible: sensitive
[4] faire l'école buissonnière: to play truant

Questions

1. *(a)* How did Stéphane die? **1 point**

   (b) He phoned his parents three days before he died.
   Why was his death completely unexpected? **3 points**

2. *(a)* Why are his parents so intent on finding out what went wrong? **2 points**

   (b) Why are they not ashamed to admit that their son was a drug addict? **2 points**

3. *(a)* What are we told about his work at school and his school friends? **2 points**

   (b) Why did he play truant? **1 point**

   (c) According to his parents, why was sending him to a boarding school a bad idea? **1 point**

4. *(a)* Why was he expelled from his new school? **1 point**

   (b) Why did his parents have no success in talking to him? **1 point**

5. *(a)* What did he do after leaving school? **1 point**

   (b) How did he cope when he split up with his girlfriend? **1 point**

   (c) What happened in February? **2 points**

   (d) Why was he hospitalised? **2 points**

6. *(a)* Why do his parents think he phoned prior to his death? **1 point**

   (b) How did they find out that he had died? **1 point**

22 points

EDUCATION AND WORK

Passage 4

Grégory — pompier volontaire

Grégory, 15 ans, enfile sa tenue[1] de pompier au moins deux fois par semaine. A la caserne des JSP (jeunes sapeurs-pompiers) dans la région parisienne, il retrouve ses copains, garçons et filles âgés de 12 à 16 ans. Pour Grégory, *"les pompiers, c'est une grande famille"*. Une famille qu'il a rejointe il y a trois ans: après un accident de vélo, il est
5   ramassé par un pompier qui lui demande ce qu'il aimerait faire plus tard. Quelle question! Sapeur-pompier! On lui donne donc l'adresse de la caserne la plus proche de chez lui. Remis de son accident, Grégory rédige une lettre expliquant pourquoi il veut devenir sapeur-pompier, il passe un entretien et le tour est joué!

Avec d'autres jeunes Grégory apprend comment agir en cas d'incendie. *"Les filles sont*
10   *moins nombreuses, mais elles ont du cran"*[2], reconnaît-il. Pour monter sur une échelle de 30 mètres, ou pour transporter les lances d'incendie, il faut être motivé! *"La première fois qu'on a fait semblant d'éteindre une voiture en feu, j'ai trouvé ça dur,* raconte Grégory. *En voyant les pneus éclater, j'ai plongé par terre de surprise. Le contraire de ce qu'il fallait faire!"* Les JSP sont chronométrés[3] dans les exercices pour s'entraîner à aller le plus vite
15   possible. Mais ils n'éteignent jamais d'incendie, c'est trop dangereux.

Grégory et ses copains font aussi beaucoup de secourisme[4], car en cas d'accident, de malaise ou d'asphyxie, c'est les pompiers qu'on appelle. Ils apprennent à transporter une victime qui s'est fracturé la colonne vertébrale, à cisailler des carcasses de voitures dans lesquelles des personnes sont coincées, à ranimer des asphyxiés . . . Tous ces scénarios sont
20   répétés avec des mannequins, ou bien l'un des JSP joue les cobayes, maquillés en victime sanguinolente[5], pour faire plus vrai!

Grégory et son équipe de jeunes sapeurs-pompiers sont champions de France. L'année dernière, les onze jeunes sauveteurs ont remporté avec succès les compétitions d'incendie et de secourisme, ainsi que les épreuves sportives. En effet, en plus des manœuvres, les JSP
25   font du sport au moins une fois par semaine: course, natation . . . histoire de garder la forme! Pour célébrer leur victoire, ils ont organisé une soirée entre pompiers, à la caserne. Musique, barbecue, déguisement[6] . . . Une fête de plus parmi toutes celles qu'ils font ensemble. Cette ambiance, Grégory ne la quitterait pour rien au monde. D'ailleurs, il passe généralement toutes ses vacances scolaires chez les pompiers. Il s'entraîne, regarde
30   travailler les adultes et participe, comme tout le monde, aux tâches du quotidien: ménage, peinture, réparations . . .

Grégory passera le brevet de pompier volontaire quand il aura 16 ans. Pour l'obtenir, il travaille sérieusement. Chaque jour, en plus de ses devoirs de collège, il apprend ses cours de secourisme ou révise les grades. Il lui arrive d'ailleurs souvent de ne pas pouvoir sortir
35 avec ses copains parce qu'il a "*la caserne à réviser*", comme il dit. Mais il ne s'en plaint pas. Il n'a qu'un but: devenir pompier de Paris.

[1] une tenue: a uniform
[2] avoir du cran: to have guts
[3] chronométrer: to time
[4] le secourisme: first aid
[5] sanguinolent: covered with blood
[6] le déguisement: fancy dress

Questions

1. *(a)* Who exactly are the "jeunes sapeurs-pompiers"?   **2 points**

    (b) What happened to Grégory three years ago which perhaps prompted his desire to become a fireman?   **3 points**

    (c) How was he selected?   **2 points**

2. *(a)* Grégory thinks that the girls have guts. What two examples does he give which highlight their motivation?   **2 points**

    (b) What happened during his first simulated car-burning exercise?   **2 points**

    (c) Why do the JSP never put out real fires?   **1 point**

3. *(a)* In their first aid classes what do the JSP learn to do?   **3 points**

    (b) How do they practise these scenarios?   **2 points**

4. *(a)* Which sports are practised by the JSP?   **2 points**

    (b) What does Grégory do at the station during his holidays?   **3 points**

5. *(a)* Why is he sometimes unable to go out with his friends?   **1 point**

    (b) Why does he not mind?   **1 point**

                                24 points

Passage 5

Lycéen du bout du monde

Lundi, 8 heures. Jason s'enferme dans sa chambre devant son émetteur-récepteur radio[1] pour sa première leçon de la journée: 30 minutes de physique. «Hello, Miss Burt» articule-t-il dans son micro. Une voix lointaine lui répond «Hello Jason, how are you today?» Jason est australien. Comme tous les jeunes qui vivent dans le désert, il prend des cours par radio
5 avec l' « école de l'air». Chaque matin, entre 8h et 12h, il retrouve avec 9 autres lycéens, la voix de Miss Burt, puis celle de ses autres professeurs, par tranches de 30 minutes. Une fois par semaine, il a droit à 10 minutes de cours particuliers, pour tester son niveau et ses connaissances.

Le ranch où il vit avec sa famille est à plus de 1 000 km d'Alice Springs, l'une des 13
10 «écoles de l'air» australiennes qui, avec ses 140 élèves, couvre une superficie[2] plus grande que celle de l'Europe. Jason a peu d'amis, le ranch le plus proche étant à 150 km de chez lui. Alors, deux ou trois fois par an, il part une semaine à Alice Springs pour voir ses professeurs et mettre un visage sur les voix de ses copains de classe. Discuter de ses difficultés, de ses espoirs, se renseigner sur la formation qu'il peut suivre après . . . une fois
15 par an, sa prof principale vient le voir, en avion ou en voiture. Elle vient passer un week-end, comme une amie. En début d'année scolaire, il reçoit ses manuels et tous les 15 jours, par courrier, des vidéos d'exercices et des devoirs à faire. Évidemment, dans un sens comme dans l'autre, la ponctualité est aléatoire[3]. S'il pleut, l'avion ne peut pas décoller, donc il ne reçoit pas de courrier.

20 Parfois, Jason manque ses cours: quand il part faire du « mustering» avec son père et les cow-boys australiens. Pendant une semaine, il parcourt le ranch (600 km), à cheval, en voiture ou même en hélicoptère, pour regrouper les bêtes, les marquer, les soigner. A son retour, complètement désorienté[4], il commence par raconter ses aventures à ses copains avant d'attaquer son cours d'histoire-géo. Après ses cours radio, il déjeune rapidement
25 avec sa mère et Alicia, sa petite sœur. Jason se débrouille tout seul, travaille devant la vidéo pour faire ses devoirs et file monter «Duchesse», son cheval, qu'il a dressé lui-même. Quand le soleil se couche, c'est l'heure où la terre devient rouge et où les kangourous sortent pour se nourrir. Jason s'exerce aussi au lancer du boomerang, pour arriver un jour à chasser les oiseaux . . .

30 Jason est en dernière année de l' «école de l'air». Après ses examens qu'il passe à Alice Springs, il ira à l'université de Melbourne ou de Sydney, pour apprendre l'agriculture. Et en même temps s'amuser et se faire des copains. A la fin de ses études, il voudrait se marier et revenir ici, au ranch. C'est la vie de Bushman qui lui plaît.

[1] un émetteur-récepteur radio : a transmitter-receiver radio
[2] une superficie: an area
[3] aléatoire: uncertain
[4] désorienté: disorientated

Questions

1. Jason does not go to school in the conventional way.

   (a) How does he learn? **1 point**

   (b) What happens once a week? **2 points**

2. *(a)* Why does Jason have few friends? **1 point**

   (b) How often does he meet up with his teachers and school friends in Alice Springs? **1 point**

   (c) What does he discuss with them? **3 points**

3. *(a)* What happens at the start of the school year? **1 point**

   (b) What happens if it rains? **2 points**

4. *(a)* What exactly does Jason do to the livestock when he is "mustering"? **3 points**

   (b) How does Jason do his homework? **1 point**

   (c) What happens at sunset? **2 points**

   (d) Why is Jason practising his boomerang throw? **1 point**

5. *(a)* What is he hoping to do after his exams? **2 points**

   (b) What is he hoping to do while he is studying? **2 points**

   (c) Why does he want to return to his ranch with his wife? **1 point**

   23 points

THE WIDER WORLD

Passage 6

Coup de pouce[1]

Adama est un grand garçon timide de 18 ans. Il vit avec sa famille, son frère et ses trois sœurs, à Ouagadougou, la capitale du Burkina-Faso. Jusqu'à ces derniers mois, Adama n'avait jamais mis les pieds dans une école. Ses journées, il les passait avec son oncle aveugle qui mendiait dans les rues. Aujourd'hui, Adama apprend la menuiserie dans un
5   centre de formation professionnelle[2]. C'est lui qui a choisi ce métier, bien qu'il n'ait jamais travaillé le bois auparavant. Adama, comme les autres jeunes du centre, apprendra à lire et à écrire pendant sa formation.

A 13 ans, Mariam n'est jamais allée à l'école, elle non plus. Ici, au centre, elle a choisi la couture. Avec ses copines, elle travaille sur des machines Singer qui ont beaucoup vécu.
10   Pas de temps à perdre, une entreprise vient de commander des blouses au centre de formation.

Avec ses cheveux savamment coiffés en arrière, sa copine Bintou a choisi la mécanique auto. Dans son bleu de travail tout maculé de[3] graisse, au milieu de la cour ensoleillée, elle a déjà l'air d'une vraie "pro". L'ambition de Bintou est d'ouvrir plus tard son propre atelier
15   de réparation de Mobylette. Le travail ne devrait pas manquer tant les Burkinabés[4] sont fans des deux-roues.

Le centre de formation où Adama, Bintou, Mariam et une soixantaine de jeunes (dont un tiers de filles) apprennent un vrai métier n'est pas un centre ordinaire. Il est réservé aux enfants les plus pauvres, ceux qui passent leur journée dans la rue et rentrent dans leur
20   famille (quand ils en ont encore une . . .) juste pour dormir.

Les fondateurs du centre ont sillonné[5] la ville pour sélectionner leurs futurs élèves. Ce projet, aidé financièrement par l'Unicef, a pris le beau nom de "Coup de pouce". Un vrai coup de pouce en effet à des jeunes "largués" par le système scolaire et qui ne savent rien faire, ou presque.

25   «Or le Burkina manque de professionnels qualifiés, explique le directeur du centre. A nous de les former en un peu plus de deux ans. Nos jeunes ne manquent pas d'ambition. Ils veulent être leur propre patron.»

Quand il sera un artisan prospère, dans son propre atelier, Adama le menuisier pourra enfin entrer dans un cinéma. Jusqu'ici, ce gaillard de 18 ans n'a jamais eu assez d'argent pour se
30   payer le prix d'une place. Une simple place de cinéma à 1,50 franc.

[1]   un coup de pouce: a helping hand
[2]   un centre de formation professionnelle: a professional training centre
[3]   maculé de: covered with
[4]   les Burkinabés: the inhabitants of Burkina-Faso
[5]   sillonner: to cover the length and breadth of

Questions

1. (a) Mention three personal details about Adama.   **3 points**

    (b) How did he used to spend his days?   **2 points**

    (c) While Adama is doing his training, what else will he learn?   **2 points**

2. Why does Mariam have to work so hard at present?   **2 points**

3. (a) What has Bintou chosen as her training?   **1 point**

    (b) What is her ambition?   **1 point**

    (c) Why should she never be short of work?   **1 point**

4. (a) What is the boy-girl ratio in the training centre?   **1 point**

    (b) For whom is the centre really intended?   **3 points**

5. (a) In what way are these young people helping the country?   **1 point**

    (b) How long does their training last?   **2 points**

    (c) What ambition do these young people have?   **1 point**

6. (a) What will Adama be able to do once he has his own workshop?   **1 point**

    (b) Why has he never done this before?   **1 point**

    (c) What are we told in the final sentence which highlights the extent of his
         poverty?   **2 points**

                                                                                        24 points

ANSWER SCHEMES

Passage 1

Appel à la tolérance

1. (a) If you were to see Pierre in the street, what wrong conclusion might you draw? **2 points**
   - he had been drinking
   - he had been taking drugs
   - he is contagious
     (any 2)

   (b) Why would he be in this state? **1 point**
   - he would have just had an epileptic fit

2. (a) What were the first symptoms 14 years ago? **2 points**
   - feeling faint (dizzy)(discomfort)
   - blackouts (fainting fits)

   (b) Mention two other symptoms which developed later. **2 points**
   - violent attacks
   - severe headaches
   - loss of memory
   - running away
     (any 2)

   (c) Why did his friends turn their backs on him? **2 points**
   - they thought his illness was contagious
   - or that he had given up alcohol and these were the effects

3. (a) Why was the situation especially difficult for his children? **2 points**
   - they wanted to go out and play
   - or do sport with their parents

   (b) What ultimatum did Fabienne finally give her husband? **1 point**
   - to go out with her or stay in without her

4. (a) What happens when someone has an epileptic fit? **3 points**
   - muscles become tense
   - eyes roll in their sockets
   - the person foams at the mouth

   (b) How do they feel after the fit? **2 points**
   - exhausted
   - as if they had been skiing non-stop for two days

5.   Why were two policemen suspicious of Pierre?   **1 point**
     • they thought he had been injecting drugs in the public toilets

6.   Pierre tries to lead a normal, healthy life. What two things does he do?   **2 points**
     • he sees to the garden
     • he prepares meals

7.   How does Tony's daily routine begin?   **1 point**
     • he washes and shaves

8.   What advice is given if you are present when someone is having a fit?   **3 points**
     • do not lift the person
     • give him / her nothing to drink
     • keep any objects out of his / her reach
     • help him / her to breathe freely
     • call an ambulance, chemist or doctor
       (any 3)

                                                                                     24 points

                                                                          (Unit award 15 / 24)

Pasage 2

Dans la peau d'un SDF

1. Who make up the 200 000 homeless people? **3 points**
   - large majority of single men
   - homeless women
   - more and more under 25s

2. *(a)* Why does Bertrand find the winters so hard? **2 points**
   - he shivers the whole night in the wind
   - trying to heat himself up in a coat full of holes
   - it makes him ill and tires him even more
     (any 2)

   (b) Why is he unable to sleep in the entrance hall of a block of flats? **1 point**
   - he is thrown out by the caretakers

   (c) What happened once when he tried to sleep in a shopping centre? **1 point**
   - the night watchmen hit him

   (d) Why does he not like sleeping at a refuge centre? **3 points**
   - there are too many people in the same dormitory
   - there are fights
   - he has even had his shoes stolen

3. Several organisations serve hot meals. Where does most of the food come from? **1 point**
   - European Union stocks

4. *(a)* As a child why did Julien sometimes feel like leaving home? **1 point**
   - he was afraid
   OR
   - he was physically abused

   (b) He feels imprisoned on the street. What keeps him trapped? **1 point**
   - his bad memories

5. Mention three things we are told about his father. **3 points**
   - his father drank
   - he came home drunk almost every evening
   - he beat Julien (for no reason)

6. How did Julien's wife end their relationship?   **1 point**
    - she threw him out of their flat

7. What does he say about the cheap wine that he drinks?   **1 point**
    - it is the worst companion he has ever had

8. *(a)* What do passers-by generally do when Jean-Marc begs?   **2 points**
    - they march past as if he did not exist
    - they rarely speak
    - far less smile
      (any 2)

    (b) What comment might they make?   **2 points**
    - find a job
    - instead of staying on the street

                                                                                      22 points

                                                                                 (Unit award 14 / 22)

Passage 3

Le danger de la drogue

1. (a) How did Stéphane die?   **1 point**
         • a drug overdose

    (b) He phoned his parents three days before he died.   **3 points**
         Why was his death completely unexpected?
         • he said he was coming out of hospital
         • and that all was well
         • that he was on his way back home
         • that his parents needn't worry
         • that he had finished with drugs (he had moved on)
           (any 3)

2. (a) Why are his parents so intent on finding out what went wrong?   **2 points**
         • so that other young people do not end up the same way
         • so that parents do not have to go through the same thing

    (b) Why are they not ashamed to admit that their son was a drug addict?   **2 points**
         • they want to break the taboo
         • and show that it can happen to anyone

3. (a) What are we told about his work at school and his school friends?   **2 points**
         • he got quite bad results
         • his friends left a lot to be desired

    (b) Why did he play truant?   **1 point**
         • to go fishing

    (c) According to his parents, why was sending him to a boarding school a bad idea?   **1 point**
         • Stéphane probably felt rejected

4. (a) Why was he expelled from his new school?   **1 point**
         • for sniffing glue

    (b) Why did his parents have no success in talking to him?   **1 point**
         • he did not listen to them

5.   *(a)*   What did he do after leaving school?   **1 point**
- he found a job as an apprentice cook (chef)

       (b)   How did he cope when he split up with his girlfriend?   **1 point**
- he found refuge and comfort in alcohol and drugs

       (c)   What happened in February?   **2 points**
- he and a friend broke a shop window
- to steal glue

       (d)   Why was he hospitalised?   **2 points**
- he was found in a coma
- in the middle of the street

6.   *(a)*   Why do his parents think he phoned prior to his death?   **1 point**
- to reassure them

       (b)   How did they find out that he had died?   **1 point**
- a policeman came to the door

22 points

(Unit award 14 / 22)

Passage 4

Grégory — pompier volontaire

1.   *(a)*   Who exactly are the "jeunes sapeurs-pompiers"?   **2 points**
   - boys and girls between the ages of 12 and 16
   - who are training to be firemen and women

    (b)   What happened to Grégory three years ago which perhaps prompted his desire to become a fireman?   **3 points**
   - he had a cycling accident
   - he was picked up by a fireman
   - who gave him the address of the nearest fire station

    (c)   How was he selected?   **2 points**
   - he wrote a letter explaining why he wanted to become a fireman
   - he had an interview

2.   *(a)*   Grégory thinks that the girls have guts. What two examples does he give which highlight their motivation?   **2 points**
   - climbing a ladder 30 metres high
   - carrying fire hoses

    (b)   What happened during his first simulated car-burning exercise?   **2 points**
   - Grégory dived to the ground in surprise
   - when the tyres burst

    (c)   Why do the JSP never put out real fires?   **1 point**
   - it is too dangerous

3.   *(a)*   In their first aid classes what do the JSP learn to do?   **3 points**
   - to transport someone who has broken his / her spine
   - to cut into car frames in which people are trapped
   - to resuscitate victims of asphyxiation

    (b)   How do they practise these scenarios?   **2 points**
   - they use dummies
   - or one of the JSP is used as a guinea-pig

4. *(a)* Which sports are practised by the JSP?   **2 points**
- running
- swimming

(b) What does Grégory do at the station during his holidays?   **3 points**
- he trains
- he watches the adults at work
- he takes part in the daily chores: housework, painting and repairs

5. *(a)* Why is he sometimes unable to go out with his friends?   **1 point**
- he has to revise for the fire service

(b) Why does he not mind?   **1 point**
- he has only one goal in mind: to become a Paris fireman

                                                                                        24 points

(Unit award 15 / 24)

Passage 5

Lycéen du bout du monde

1. Jason does not go to school in the conventional way.

    (a) How does he learn?   **1 point**
        • using a transmitter-receiver radio

    (b) What happens once a week?   **2 points**
        • he can have a 10-minute lesson with a teacher on his own
        • to test his level of attainment and knowledge

2. (a) Why does Jason have few friends?   **1 point**
        • the nearest ranch is 150 km away from his home

    (b) How often does he meet up with his teachers and school friends in Alice Springs?   **1 point**
        • two or three times a year

    (c) What does he discuss with them?   **3 points**
        • his difficulties
        • his hopes
        • he finds out about the training (course) he can do later

3. (a) What happens at the start of the school year?   **1 point**
        • he receives his textbooks

    (b) What happens if it rains?   **2 points**
        • the plane cannot take off
        • so he does not receive any mail

4. (a) What exactly does Jason do to the livestock when he is "mustering"?   **3 points**
        • he regroups the animals
        • he marks them
        • he looks after them

    (b) How does Jason do his homework?   **1 point**
        • in front of the video

(c) What happens at sunset?   **2 points**
- the land turns red
- the kangaroos come out to feed

(d) Why is Jason practising his boomerang throw?   **1 point**
- so that he can hunt birds one day

5.   *(a)* What is he hoping to do after his exams?   **2 points**
- to go to university
- to study agriculture

(b) What is he hoping to do while he is studying?   **2 points**
- to have fun
- to make friends

(c) Why does he want to return to his ranch with his wife?   **1 point**
- a bushman's life appeals to him

23 points

(Unit award 14 / 23)

Passage 6

Coup de pouce

1. *(a)* Mention three personal details about Adama.   **3 points**
    - tall, shy, 18 years old (any 1)
    - lives with his family (one brother, three sisters)
    - lives in Ouagadougou (capital of Burkina-Faso)

    (b) How did he used to spend his days?   **2 points**
    - with his blind uncle
    - who begged in the street

    (c) While Adama is doing his training, what else will he learn?   **2 points**
    - to read
    - to write

2. Why does Mariam have to work so hard at present?   **2 points**
    - a company has just put in an order
    - for overalls from the training centre

3. *(a)* What has Bintou chosen as her training?   **1 point**
    - car mechanics

    (b) What is her ambition?   **1 point**
    - to open her own moped-repair workshop

    (c) Why should she never be short of work?   **1 point**
    - the inhabitants of Burkina-Faso are moped fans
      (mopeds are very popular there)

4. *(a)* What is the boy / girl ratio in the training centre?   **1 point**
    - 1 / 3 girls

    (b) For whom is the centre really intended?   **3 points**
    - the poorest children
    - those who spend the day on the street
    - and go home to their families (if they have one) just to sleep

5.   *(a)*   In what way are these young people helping the country?   **1 point**
- Burkina has a shortage of skilled workers

     (b)   How long does their training last?   **2 points**
- just over
- two years

     (c)   What ambition do these young people have?   **1 point**
- to be their own boss

6.   *(a)*   What will Adama be able to do once he has his own workshop?   **1 point**
- go to a cinema

     (b)   Why has he never done this before?   **1 point**
- he has never had enough money

     (c)   What are we told in the final sentence which highlights the extent of his poverty?   **2 points**
- a cinema ticket
- only costs 1,50F

24 points

(Unit award 15 / 24)

RECORD OF ACHIEVEMENT

The following can be used to record your marks and will help you to monitor your own progress.

READING

Lifestyles	Questions (20)	Translation (10)	Total Mark (30)
Passage 1			
Passage 2			
Passage 3			
Passage 4			
Passage 5			

Education & Work	Questions (20)	Translation (10)	Total Mark (30)
Passage 6			
Passage 7			
Passage 8			
Passage 9			
Passage 10			
Passage 11			

The Wider World	Questions (20)	Translation (10)	Total Mark (30)
Passage 12			
Passage 13			
Passage 14			
Passage 15			

DIRECTED WRITING

	Mark out of 15		*Mark out of 15*
Directed Writing 1		Directed Writing 6	
Directed Writing 2		Directed Writing 7	
Directed Writing 3		Directed Writing 8	
Directed Writing 4		Directed Writing 9	
Directed Writing 5		Directed Writing 10	

END OF UNIT READING

Lifestyles	*mark*	*unit award*	*pass/fail*
Passage 1	/ 24	15 / 24	
Passage 2	/ 22	14 / 22	
Passage 3	/ 22	14 / 22	
Education & Work			
Passage 4	/ 24	15 / 24	
Passage 5	/ 23	14 / 23	
The Wider World			
Passage 6	/ 24	15 / 24	